AF255714

"As a leading expert in the church's role in suicide prevention, Karen Mason has compiled a tremendously helpful resource on the 'essential elements' for the church's role in preserving the lives of suicidal individuals. This book will be invaluable for church leaders who want to provide a skillful, compassionate, and life-affirming response to people's suffering and distress."

—**Curtis Lehmann**, licensed psychologist, Center for Flourishing

"*The Essentials of Suicide Prevention* is an essential resource for pastoral leaders. Karen Mason's research and insights thoroughly integrate the disciplines of theology and psychology, duly recognizing the purpose and mission of the church as an important part of preventive care and holistic health. Church leaders will be simultaneously informed and inspired as this book raises awareness and better equips leaders to serve this present age via the life-affirming hope of the gospel."

—**C. Guy Robinson**, pastor, Tabernacle of the Lord Church

"Persons experiencing suicidal desperation are often considered sick people who need to be fixed so they can fit into the faith community again. *The Essentials of Suicide Prevention* takes an important step in the opposite direction: changing faith communities to become places where the suicidally desperate find remedies to issues that made them desperate in the first place."

—**Fe Anam Avis**, author of *A Second Day: A Hopeful Journey out of Suicidal Thinking*

"*The Essentials of Suicide Prevention* is a gift to the church. In a winsome, well-researched, and accessible way, Mason engages with one of the most slippery areas of ministry in which a church can take part—suicide prevention. There isn't a person in a congregation who hasn't been affected by suicide. The 'essentials' in this helpful book provide concrete steps for suicide prevention that any church can implement and from which any church can benefit."

—**Scott M. Gibson**, George W. Truett Theological Seminary

"After reading this work my immediate reaction was to rise to action. Karen Mason's careful and expert research on the topic not only illumines the problem (stigmas and a faulty anthropology) but provides a doable way forward for the church. In this case, reading and following the blueprint she offers truly is a matter of life or death."

—**Donna Petter**, Gordon-Conwell Theological Seminary

"*The Essentials for Suicide Prevention* is a must-read for clergy and other leaders who want to stop being observers and take action in helping those who may be suicidal. Through her extensive research, Mason provides encouraging resources that will make measurable differences in the well-being of its members and visitors."

—**Jeff Elhart**, Executive Committee member, National Action Alliance for Suicide Prevention

The Essentials of Suicide Prevention

The Essentials of Suicide Prevention

—— A Blueprint for Churches ——

Karen Mason

CASCADE *Books* · Eugene, Oregon

THE ESSENTIALS OF SUICIDE PREVENTION
A Blueprint for Churches

Copyright © 2023 Karen Mason. All rights reserved. Except for brief quotations in critical publications or reviews, no part of this book may be reproduced in any manner without prior written permission from the publisher. Write: Permissions, Wipf and Stock Publishers, 199 W. 8th Ave., Suite 3, Eugene, OR 97401.

Cascade Books
An Imprint of Wipf and Stock Publishers
199 W. 8th Ave., Suite 3
Eugene, OR 97401

www.wipfandstock.com

PAPERBACK ISBN: 978-1-6667-0976-6
HARDCOVER ISBN: 978-1-6667-0977-3
EBOOK ISBN: 978-1-6667-0978-0

Cataloguing-in-Publication data:

Names: Mason, Karen, 1955–, author.

Title: The essentials of suicide prevention : a blueprint for churches / by Karen Mason.

Description: Eugene, OR : Cascade Books, 2023 | Includes bibliographical references.

Identifiers: ISBN 978-1-6667-0976-6 (paperback) | ISBN 978-1-6667-0977-3 (hardcover) | ISBN 978-1-6667-0978-0 (ebook)

Subjects: LCSH: Suicide—Religious aspects—Christianity. | Pastoral counseling.

Classification: BV4012.2 .M297 2023 (print) | BV4012.2 .M297 (ebook)

01/19/23

Scriptures taken from the Holy Bible, New International Version®, NIV®. Copyright © 1973, 1978, 1984, 2011, by Biblica, Inc.TM Used by permission of Zondervan. All rights reserved worldwide. www.zondervan.com The "NIV" and "New International Version" are trademarks registered in the United States Patent and Tradmark Office by Biblica, Inc. TM

Material reproduced from Scott Gibson and Karen Mason, *Preaching Hope in Darkness: Help for Pastors in Addressing Suicide from the Pulpit* (Bellingham, WA: Lexham Press, 2020) is used here by permission.

To Cher and Scott, who gave me a safe haven for writing the book

Contents

Acknowledgments

The bold members of the National Action Alliance for Suicide Prevention Faith Communities Task Force dare to talk about suicide prevention in faith communities. Some of their stories are included in the book. Their courage to change the conversation about suicide in faith communities and their perseverance in finding ways for churches to do suicide prevention have inspired the book. Heartfelt thanks to Gordon-Conwell Theological Seminary trustees and administration for their generous sabbatical leave, to the library staff for their help with locating resources, and to my two remarkable students who helped with research and the formatting of the book: Zihan Yang and Bellanira Rynbrandt.

Introduction

Choose life. (Deut 30:19)

Is Suicide Preventable?

THE US SUICIDE RATE has steadily climbed from 29,199 deaths in 1999 to 48,344 in 2018, a similar number to those who died by an opioid overdose in 2018.[1] Suicide is a problem in the US. And it is a visible tragedy not only in society, but also in the church.

On April 5, 2013, Matthew Warren took his life. If Matthew had grown up in your church, what would you do? His parents, co-founders of Saddleback Church, grieved and continue to grieve. And his mother, Kay Warren, rallied her community to develop Be Well Orange County[2] to make sure that everyone who needed care got care, to prevent suicide. "Prevent suicide?" you might ask. "Is it possible to prevent suicide?"

You may be asking the question because you worry about a loved one's thoughts of suicide, or you have lost a loved one to suicide. You ask, "Are there signs I can look for or signs that I missed? Can I prevent a suicide?" Matthew had distressing thoughts of suicide ever since he was a child. Mental health challenges were a life-long struggle for him. His parents had feared he might one day take his life. Olya had agonizing thoughts of suicide ever since she was eight years old. For years she struggled until, in her early twenties, she couldn't leave the house, paralyzed by anxiety. She reached out for help, and after counseling, she now works on a suicide hotline. Both Olya and Matthew had similar signs, but one died and the other did not. Suicide is hard to predict, and the signs

1. In 2018, 46,802 Americans died of an opioid overdose. Hedegaard et al., *Drug Overdose Deaths.*

2. See their website: https://bewelloc.org/.

of suicide don't do a good job of predicting who will die by suicide.[3] But just because suicide is hard to predict does not mean it's not preventable.[4] Olya's suicide was prevented. It was prevented when she reached out to a trusted college professor who connected her to a psychiatrist and a counselor. People came together to help her.

Some suicides are preventable—by trained professionals like professors, psychiatrists, and counselors. But what about ordinary Christians in an ordinary church? What about pastors who often are not trained in suicide intervention? What can we do? This book will lay out eight tools for suicide prevention that any church can carry out. But there is one tool we must begin with. The first tool is our belief that God is the healer. Believing that God is the healer gives courage to untrained and trained Christians alike.

God Is the Healer

In the book of Psalms, we read that God is the healer of all our diseases (Ps 103:3). Regardless of your doctor's skill in curing your poison ivy or Lymes disease or cancer, it is God who ultimately heals. It's a simple Christian belief, but a comforting one to both trained and untrained Christians. "God is the healer" means that we, trained or untrained, show up with everything we have but God himself is the ultimate healer. Suicide prevention isn't something that we do on our own. We are partnering with God himself.

Of course, you might ask, "Why doesn't God heal everyone? Why did Matthew die by suicide?" I wish I had an answer to that question. It's the same question that Job asked God. As we read through Job 38–41, what's striking is that God never answers that question. He says, "I am God," an answer that calls us to have faith in him.

We don't have all the answers we'd like to have, but we are not on our own in this task of suicide prevention. We have God's healing presence. We also have the church community.

3. See Alpert, "Is Suicide Preventable?"

4. See "Is Suicide Preventable?"

God's Presence in Churches

Regular church attendance helps prevent suicide.[5] What is it about churches that decreases the likelihood of suicide? Some have said that social support in a church is what helps.[6] Belonging to any group will help a suicidal person. For example, a book club or sports team can help. But what is uniquely powerful in a Christian faith community is participating with a group that shares your faith convictions, that shares your unique common interest in faith.[7] But churches are more than common interest groups. Churches are inhabited by God himself. The people of Israel saw God's glory fill the Tabernacle (Exod 40:34) and the Temple (2 Chr 7:1). Churches today are the Temple of the Holy Spirit (1 Cor 3:16). And God's presence is life-giving. As one pastor said it:

> We can live as [Jesus'] hands and feet, incarnate in the world, bringing redemption and healing to others in his Name and in his power. This is why the church is not a club—we're not just gathered over common interests, or even common belief. We meet together because we have the assurance that when we do, God is present—his life and vitality are present. I don't need to heal people, I don't need to save people—if I can bring people into proximity of Jesus, I believe he will do his work—because he has entered the world—our time and space. When the church really understands its identity as the community of the incarnate Lord, where Jesus walks among us, and leads us, and brings people to us—I think we would all see our work in the world in a very different way. Jesus asks us to believe in him—to receive him, and do the works he gives us to do.[8]

The gospel is a message of life, not death. Church is a place where God's presence is a vital force for life. It is in communities of faith that Christians gather to share God's healing presence with each other. While not all churches automatically incarnate God's life-giving presence, churches can be the hands and feet of the healing God to those struggling with wanting to stay alive.

5. Koenig et al., *Handbook of Religion and Health*; VanderWeele et al., *Religious Service Attendance and Lower Suicide Rates*.

6. Joiner, *Why People Die by Suicide*; LaPierre, *Model for Describing Spirituality*.

7. Mason et al., *Unique Experiences in Religious Groups*.

8. Sermon delivered by the Rev. Canon Jay L. Greener on Sunday, December 30, 2018, Church of the Redeemer, Highwood, IL. Printed with his permission.

God's presence in churches is a unique force in suicide prevention. But pastors and congregants have even more to offer people struggling with suicidal thoughts.

Choose Life and Have Hope

At a suicide prevention conference, I heard two experts on a panel. One was asked why a person should stay alive. The expert hemmed and hawed. He couldn't answer the question. Science can't answer that question. To answer that question, you need the Bible. The Bible tells us to choose life (Deut 30:19) because God is the giver of life (Job 1:21; 1 Tim 6:13), the sustainer of all life (Col 1:17) and the lover of each life (John 3:16). Jesus valued all life. He showed love to everyone, including tax collectors (Luke 19:1–10), outcast lepers (Luke 17:11–19) and an adulterous, ostracized Samaritan woman (John 4:1–42).

Christians firmly believe in the sanctity of every human life. When Christians speak about "the sanctity of life," that applies not only to the life of a pre-born infant, but also to the life of every human being, regardless of their situation. As a psychologist, I have met many people who believe they are unworthy to live. They worry that they are damaged goods or a burden to their family. The voice in their head tells them "You're such a failure," and "Why don't you have your life together yet?" But *all* people, regardless of their situation, have worth and dignity because they are created in the image of God (Gen 1:28–29; Pss 8, 139:14). People struggling with wanting to live need to know that their lives matter, that their worth doesn't depend on anything but God's love for them, that they come to God as they are, that they don't need to "clean up" before coming to church. The sanctity of every human life is the basic foundation for suicide prevention. This Christian belief speaks clearly into a person's desire for death. It is this clarity that makes church involvement in suicide prevention so vital.

But there is more. What is striking in the Bible is how over and over God redeems hopeless situations. Joseph was sold into slavery, he landed in prison for years, but he ended up saving his family from famine. Israel was exiled but returned to the Promised Land. Jesus died and he rose again. In these narratives, God gives us hope in the midst of great suffering. Hope is a unique contribution of people of faith to suicide prevention. Hopeless people in the midst of depression, job loss, or relationship loss can find hope because God is present (Ps 34:18), sovereign (Job 42:2;

Ps 31:15), loving (1 John 4:8), and mighty to save (Zeph 3:17; 1 Cor 6:14). We can have the certainty that, as the prophet Joel says, God will repay the years that the locusts have eaten (Joel 2:25). And we won't be ashamed of having held onto this hope (Rom 5:5).

You may be saying to yourself, "This is all fine and good, but I'm no theologian. What can an ordinary Christian like me do?" This theology translates into what we Christians do every day in ordinary churches.

The Implications

God's clear value of all life has implications for every Christian today, as it did for the Apostle Paul in Philippi. There, a Roman jailer had put Paul and Silas in an inner cell of a jail and fastened their feet in stocks (Acts 16:24). About midnight, a violent earthquake opened the cell door and loosened the prisoners' chains (Acts 16:26). The writer of Acts tells us, "The jailer woke up . . . drew his sword and was about to kill himself because he thought the prisoners had escaped. But Paul shouted, 'Don't harm yourself! We are all here!'" (Acts 16:27–28). Though Paul and Silas had endured awful conditions in a jail, they did not wish for the jailer's death. Paul prevented the jailer's suicide because all life has worth and dignity, even the life of a jailer.

Wouldn't it be great if we could let apostles and pastors take care of this problem of suicide? But sometimes ordinary Christians may find themselves as the trusted confidant of a suicidal person. Before becoming a psychologist, I had a friend tell me she was thinking about suicide. I panicked because I wasn't a trained helper. I wanted my friend to talk to her pastor or a counselor. But she wouldn't. She was afraid the pastor would judge her. She couldn't find a counselor she clicked with. I had to be the "Good Samaritan." Jesus told the story of the Good Samaritan when an expert in Jewish law asked Jesus, "Who is my neighbor?" (Luke 10:29). A Jewish man traveling along a desolate mountain road was attacked by robbers and left for dead by the side of the road. The man needed someone to help him, to save his life. But two religious professionals came by, took one look at him, then passed on. It was only when an outcast Samaritan stopped that the injured man's life was saved. I was the only person who knew of my friend's suicidal thoughts and I had to be the one to help her. I was thankful for God's presence with me and with her that day.

When Experts Are Not Enough

Sometimes ordinary people are the trusted confidant of a suicidal person and sometimes, in America, problems are so big that all Americans, including ordinary people, are needed. All Americans, not just heart surgeons, are being taught to eat a healthy diet and to exercise to prevent heart disease. All Americans, not just visiting nurses, are being taught "back to sleep": to put babies to sleep on their backs, to prevent Sudden Infant Death Syndrome.

When we look at the statistics on suicide in the United States, we see a problem that requires everyone's help. More Americans die by suicide each year than die by murder or HIV AIDS.[9] Even pastors are not exempt from suicide.[10]

If we're going to prevent suicide, we will need everyone's help. In a storm, a Navy captain might command "all hands on deck," meaning that all sailors are ordered to report to the ship's deck—even if the emergency isn't within the expertise of a particular sailor. What is most needed is everyone's "hands," because everyone can contribute in some way. Similarly, preventing suicide will take everyone, including ordinary Christians in ordinary churches.

Ordinary Christians Offer Their Faith

Imagine a small community on the Gulf Coast getting ready to face the threat of a hurricane. Weather reports say that the hurricane will make landfall right over a small town. Worst of all, the storm surge is expected to flood the historic downtown. The community has come together to protect the historic downtown by surrounding it with sandbags. Wouldn't it be odd if everyone in town—*except Christians*—was filling sand bags? Even more surprising, what if those Christians owned special sandbag equipment?

In some churches, that is what is happening with suicide prevention. Even though suicide is a hurricane-sized threat, we may leave suicide prevention to the experts or to groups that don't bring in a faith perspective. Non-faith-based groups (some are listed at the end of this chapter) are

9. In 2016, 44,965 Americans died of suicide and 19,362 Americans died of homicide. HIV AIDS is not even in the top twenty causes of death (Centers for Disease Control and Prevention, *WISQARS*).

10. Inland Hills (Chino, California) Lead Pastor Andrew Stoecklein died by suicide on August 25, 2018. Pastor Jarrid Wilson died by suicide September 9, 2019. Pastor Steve Austin died by suicide June 5, 2021.

crucial to suicide prevention efforts, but they may not be able to answer the question, "Why should I stay alive?" They may not help people answer where God is in the midst of abuse or loss or depression and how to value life in the face of difficult circumstances. It is the community of faith that contributes these missing pieces for people who struggle with their desire to live. It is God's people in church who can assure people thinking about suicide that their lives matter, that they can be full members of the household of God, that they belong (Eph 2:19), that God has gifted them and they can still make a meaningful contribution to the church (Rom 12:15–26), that they can reach out for help and will get the help they need. Suicidal people need ordinary people in the community of faith.

Summary

Christians want to help their loved ones and their fellow brothers and sisters in Christ stay alive. While suicides are not always predictable, some are preventable. But leaving the task of suicide prevention to the secular experts isn't workable. Christians are empowered by God's healing presence and with the answer to the question, "Why should I stay alive in the midst of my messy life?" Pastors and congregants in ordinary churches have the precious words of life and hope to share with suicidal people.

But What Do We Actually Do?

But what do the people of God in ordinary churches actually do? What are the practical steps we can take to prevent suicide? This book will help answer that question. Each chapter will provide examples of what ordinary Christians in ordinary churches are doing.

- Chapter 1 examines how to prevent suicide and examines Christian perspectives on suffering and suicide.
- Chapter 2 investigates the unique power of the church. But what in a church is so vital? A community that does not shy away from talking about the difficulties of life allows those who are struggling to reach out for help without fear of judgment. Authentic community protects susceptible folks from suicide.

- Chapter 3 discusses the importance of preaching and teaching. What can a church do to protect vulnerable people *before* they become suicidal? After we learn how to help people at risk of suicide, we might wonder, "What can we do to help protect others from becoming suicidal?" Chapter 3 helps pastors and lay teachers understand that preaching and teaching the life-affirming messages from the Bible provide additional protection against suicide.

- Chapter 4 adds the crucial contribution of worship, the communal practices of prayer, reading the Bible and singing. These practices are essential to a church-based approach to suicide prevention.

- Chapter 5 lays out how Christians can be Good Samaritans to suicidal people. Pastors and congregants untrained in mental health approaches can learn safe ways to help those who are considering suicide or who have attempted suicide. The presence and availability of Good Samaritans in every community has long been recognized as a key aspect of every suicide prevention approach.

- Chapter 6 explores ways to connect suicidal people to systems of care. Being well resourced is a key element to a suicide prevention approach.

- Chapter 7 examines ways to support those who grieve a loss by suicide. This chapter will help pastors and congregants understand how to support those who grieve a loss by suicide, and why some people who have lost a loved one to suicide decide to leave their church after a suicide. Knowing how to support one another following a suicide is another crucial part of a comprehensive approach to suicide prevention.

- Chapter 8 lays out evidence for suicide contagion (i.e., copycat suicides), then how to know who is most vulnerable to copying a suicide and how pastors and congregants can prevent such contagion. Managing contagion is another key aspect to preventing further suicides.

- The final chapter will discuss common barriers to suicide prevention in a church, especially busy pastors and busy churches already involved in many programs. A focus on culture shift, not a suicide prevention program, is an essential element of a Christian approach to suicide prevention in a church. The final chapter will pull together the themes of the book to summarize a church-based approach to preventing suicide.

Final Thoughts

Suicide prevention is a big job that requires "all hands on deck," including pastors and congregants in ordinary churches. While we've all seen the power of one passionate individual, one person alone would not be able to fill all the sandbags needed to protect a historic district and no one Christian would be able to accomplish all these tasks. It takes a whole church to protect against suicide. Any Christian reading this book will be able to put into practice any of the eight essential elements to a church-based approach to suicide prevention, but it will take a whole church to put all eight into practice.

But what if we don't prevent all suicides? Is it still worth it? Is protecting one life worth it? Protecting at least one life is the idea behind any safety measure we take. We wear seat belts, even though some people die in car accidents wearing their seat belts. Seat belts are not foolproof, but that doesn't stop us from using them, and it doesn't make them worthless. The Gulf Coast town fills sandbags to protect the downtown historic district even though the towns people don't know where the hurricane will make landfall or how bad the storm surge will be. Every sandbag is worth the effort. Even if a church has a comprehensive suicide prevention approach, someone might still take their life. But we put in place every sandbag we can. Why? Because saving one person's life is worth it.

Matthew took his life. Can we still call this book's approach *suicide prevention*? While our goal is "zero suicides,"[11] to get there we have to decrease the likelihood of suicide. One way to think about how this works is to imagine a thermometer. At the top we have a suicide-safe person and at the bottom, a suicide-unsafe person. In between, a person moving toward the top is safer; the person moving toward the bottom is less safe. The goal of a suicide prevention approach is to nudge people toward the top. How we do that is by promoting life in the many ways explored in this book.

In the next chapter, we will review what we know about suicide in the US. A plethora of information is available that can help us understand suicide and start to build a comprehensive suicide prevention approach in our churches.

11. See their website: https://zerosuicide.edc.org/.

Discussion Questions

1. How do you think Christian faith and Christian community contribute uniquely to suicide prevention?

2. What is your experience talking with suicidal persons? With a loved one following a suicide?

3. How do you think that Christians can best value life in the face of difficult conditions?

4. What suicide prevention organizations have you heard of? Why isn't there a Christian organization on this list?

   a. American Association of Suicidology (https://www.suicidology.org/)

   b. American Foundation for Suicide Prevention (https://afsp.org/)

   c. National Action Alliance for Suicide Prevention (https://theactionalliance.org/)

   d. 988 Suicide & Crisis Lifeline (https://988lifeline.org/)

   e. Suicide Prevention Resource Center (https://www.sprc.org/)

Resources

988 Suicide & Crisis Lifeline (988).[12] 988lifeline.org

12. See *Report on the National Suicide Hotline.*

Part 1: **Prevention**

CHAPTER 1

What Is *Comprehensive* Christian Suicide Prevention?

Unless the LORD builds the house, its builders labor in vain. (Ps 127:1)

A wise man built his house on the rock. The rain came down, the streams rose, and the winds blew and beat against that house; yet it did not fall, because it had its foundation on the rock. But everyone who hears these words of mine and does not put them into practice is like a foolish man who built his house on sand. The rain came down, the streams rose, and the winds blew and beat against that house, and it fell with a great crash. (Matt 7:24–27)

I MANAGED THE OFFICE of Suicide Prevention for the Colorado Department of Public Health and Environment for a couple years. As a psychologist, I knew how to help a suicidal person. But I didn't know how to help a church prevent suicide. Over the years, I have found a lot of suicide prevention tools for churches. One of the most powerful tools is to think about suicide prevention as having three distinct phases: prevention, intervention, and postvention. Preventing suicide requires all three phases, the same way constructing a church building requires many phases. In order for a church building to withstand wind and rain and to keep its occupants safe, it requires a strong foundation, a sturdy frame to hold up the roof, and safety features like smoke and CO_2 detectors. It must have all three parts. And because a building is not built in a day, these three parts are built in phases. The same is true for suicide prevention. There are many parts to suicide prevention and they are built over time. The three phases of suicide prevention are prevention (a strong foundation of a loving and safe community), intervention (a sturdy frame that assists congregants who reach out for help), and postvention (the safety features that prevent tragedy through ministering to those who have lost a loved one to suicide). Not implementing all three suicide prevention tools would be like trying to build a house without a foundation or a frame or smoke detectors.[1]

Suicide Prevention Tools

The three suicide prevention phases are important in different ways. Imagine a town where several people have drowned in the local river. In order to prevent future drownings, the town might build a fence along the river to prevent someone from falling in (prevention), or might have life jackets near the edge of the river (intervention), or the town might train lifeguards to do CPR immediately (postvention). Each is a crucial phase of prevention. Suicide prevention in a church is just as comprehensive. But what do these three phases look like for suicide prevention in churches?

Prevention

Prevention is the strong foundation of the house. Everything in the house depends on the strength of the foundation. Prevention is everything a church does that promotes life: giving people guidance about how to build lives worth living, teaching people how to manage suffering using their faith practices, providing people with wmoral objections to suicide and reasons to live, life-affirming messages woven into the fabric of the church, including in worship. These are all things that churches do naturally. Churches also need to do some things that might not come as naturally. Churches need to address the stigma of suicide directly. They need to keep in mind that suicidal people are listening to sermons. They need to offer people a community characterized by the gospel where suicidal people can reach out for help and get help. These are all part of the phase called *prevention*. Prevention requires a church to think about their attitudes about suicide,

1. The author, Karen Mason (PhD, University of Denver), is the Director of the Masters in Counseling program at the Gordon-Conwell Theological Seminary Hamilton campus and Professor of Counseling and Psychology. She is a member of the National Action Alliance for Suicide Prevention Faith Communities Task Force. She and her colleagues at Gordon-Conwell have surveyed or interviewed thousands of faith leaders and congregants about suicide prevention in faith communities, and, in the book, when she quotes "a study participant," she is referring to these many generous people who have shared their experiences with her and her colleagues.

to reflect theologically about suicide, to build a faith community that confronts suicide stigma, to offer help to people who are struggling with life, to preach and teach a theology of life, and to worship together.

Prevention is anything that a community does that promotes health and flourishing, or *shalom*. In Jeremiah 29:7, the Jewish exiles were told to "seek the *shalom* of the city to which I have carried you into exile. Pray to the Lord for it, because if it has *shalom*, you too will have *shalom*." *Shalom* is "peace and prosperity" or "welfare."[2] We are to seek the *shalom* of everyone in a church because every life is made in the image of God. Where God gives *shalom* and where people seek *shalom*, there is peace and prosperity (Ps 72:1–7), safety (Ps 4:8), healing (Isa 57:19), and good relationships between people (Gen 26:29; 1 Chr 12:17–18).

Prevention is an important part of comprehensive suicide prevention and is one of the unique contributions of the church to suicide prevention. You can read more about prevention in part 1 (chs. 1–4). In part 1, you will reflect theologically on suffering and suicide (ch. 1), you will learn how to build a safe, connected church (ch. 2), how to be a life-affirming church (ch. 3), and a worshipping church that acknowledges suicide (ch. 4).

Intervention

Intervention is the sturdy frame of the house. Each two-by-four is crucial for holding up the walls and the roof. The frame connects everything to everything else, including the power and water grid. The sturdy house frame reminds us that everyone has a role in keeping the church safe and that the church exists in a wider community. Intervention is everything that a church does to get a suicidal person help. Intervention is the phase of equipping the whole church with skills to recognize that a suicidal person is struggling. It is equipping certain people in the church with specialized skills to know what to do. It is also networking with the community to connect the suicidal person to the grid of resources in your community. This is called *intervention*. Intervention requires a church to understand their role in helping a suicidal person; it requires the church to be equipped for safety planning and referring to resources in the community.

2. VanDrunnen, *Living in Two Kingdoms*, 92. Cornelius Plantinga Jr. offers a useful definition of *shalom*: "In the Bible, *shalom* means universal flourishing, wholeness, and delight—a rich state of affairs that inspires joyful wonder as its Creator and Savior opens doors and welcomes the creatures in whom he delights" (Plantinga, *Not the Way*, 10).

Seeking the *shalom* of everyone in the church involves healing (Isa 57:19). Jesus proclaimed the kingdom of God by healing. Jesus sent his disciples to heal (Matt 10:8; Luke 9:2–6). Alleviating human suffering has always been part of the proclamation of the kingdom of God. Christians stayed in cities to care for the sick during plagues.[3] Missionaries in the nineteenth and twentieth centuries provided medical care, education, and orphanages.[4] As one of our study participants said about suicide prevention, "the lame walk, the blind see, the deaf hear."[5]

Churches are crucially important when it comes to intervention. You can read more about intervention in part 2 (chs. 5–6). In part 2, you'll learn how to build a skilled, equipped church (ch. 5) and a well-networked church (ch. 6).

Postvention

Postvention includes the safety features like smoke detectors that prevent tragedy. In a church, postvention is ministering to those who have lost a loved one to suicide and to the community as a whole. It is everything a church does when caring for a family and community following a suicide while being alert to the risks of suicide contagion. In suicide prevention, this is called *postvention*. Postvention requires pastors to learn how to conduct memorial services or memorial ceremonies, and churches how to minister to those who have lost a loved one to suicide, to manage contagion and clusters, and especially to manage one's own guilt and commit to regular Sabbath-keeping.

You can read more about postvention in part 3 (chs. 7–8). In part 3, you'll learn how to cultivate a ministering church (ch. 7) and a monitoring church (ch. 8).

A Suicide Prevention Culture

In the final chapter, you can read about how to build a suicide prevention culture, not a program. A note of caution: while it is helpful to divide suicide

---

3. Stark, "Epidemics, Networks, and the Rise of Christianity," 166.

4. Missionaries brought "the whole gospel for the whole man" (Causton, *For the Healing of the Nations*, 28).

5. Forthcoming interview from Mason et al., "How Counselors Can Help."

prevention into separate phases, you will notice throughout the book that these phases overlap because they are related to each other. It takes all three tools to prevent suicide in a church. A house needs it all: a foundation, a frame, and safety devices, and a church needs all three phases to build a culture of suicide prevention. Let's get started building a church that has a strong suicide prevention foundation by reflecting on what is powerful about church and by reflecting theologically.

Prevention: What Is Powerful in a Church

In the Introduction, we talked about what is uniquely powerful in a church: the life-giving presence of God and life-affirming beliefs in the sanctity of every human life and God's redemption of our suffering. Let's add more reasons for what makes church uniquely powerful in suicide prevention.

There are many factors[6] which increase the risk of suicide. But there are also many protective factors that lower the risk of suicide. People who go to church regularly have better physical and mental health[7] and they live longer.[8] They are less depressed.[9] People who go to church regularly have

6. Risk factors for suicide include childhood sexual abuse, interpersonal violence, firearm ownership, substance use disorders, low socioeconomic status, unemployment, chronic age, homelessness, being a veteran, immigration, sexual orientation, social isolation like being divorced, exposure to others' suicidal thinking and behavior, mental health conditions, a previous suicide attempt, problems with parents or romantic partners, and legal problems.

7. Koenig et al., *Handbook of Religion and Health*.

8. People who attend religious services at least weekly are about 30 percent less likely to die over a ten- to twenty-year follow-up: VanderWeele, "Activities for Flourishing," 85; Chida et al., "Religiosity/Spirituality and Mortality," 83; Li et al., "Religious Service Attendance and Lower Depression," 881; Li et al., "Religious Service Attendance with Mortality"; VanderWeele et al., "Religious Service Attendance and Lower Suicide Rates," 847.

9. People who attend religious services are about 30 percent less likely to become depressed: VanderWeele, "Activities for Flourishing"; Chida et al., "Religiosity/Spirituality and Mortality"; Li et al., "Religious Service Attendance and Lower Depression"; Li et al., "Religious Service Attendance with Mortality"; VanderWeele et al., "Religious Service Attendance and Lower Suicide Rates."

less suicidal thinking,[10] fewer suicide attempts,[11] and fewer suicide deaths.[12] In fact, those who attend church at least weekly are over five times less likely to die by suicide.[13] Harvard researcher Dr. Tyler J. VanderWeele believes that something powerful happens in religious services.[14]

How Does Church Protect against Suicide?

The question is what in church matters. A lot of things that happen in church are believed to make a difference. Some of these things are:

- prayer, religious coping, and religious identity[15]

- having moral objections to suicide[16]

- having reasons to live[17]

- less smoking and higher emotional well-being[18]

10. Bearman and Moody, "Suicide and Friendships"; Blackmore et al., "Psychosocial and Clinical Correlates"; Cohen et al., "Racial Differences in Suicidality"; Cook et al., "Suicidality in Older African Americans"; Greening and Stoppelbein, "Religiosity, Attributional Style, and Social Support"; Pienaar et al., "Occupational Stress."

11. Burshtein et al., "Religiosity as a Protective Factor"; Nonnemaker et al., "Public and Private Domains of Religiosity"; Thompson et al., "Delinquency and Suicidal Behaviors."

12. Barranco, "Suicide, Religion, and Latinos"; Hilton et al., "Suicide Rates and Religious Commitment"; Nisbet et al., "Effect of Participation in Religious Activities"; Chida et al., "Religiosity/Spirituality and Mortality"; Li et al., "Religious Service Attendance and Lower Depression"; Li et al., "Religious Service Attendance with Mortality"; Stack, "Effect of the Decline in Institutionalized Religion"; VanderWeele et al., "Religious Service Attendance and Lower Suicide Rates."

13. VanderWeele, "Activities for Flourishing"; Chida et al., "Religiosity/Spirituality and Mortality"; Li et al., "Religious Service Attendance and Lower Depression"; Vander-Weele et al., "Religious Service Attendance and Lower Suicide Rates."

14. VanderWeele, "Religious Communities, Health, and Well-Being."

15. Larson and Larson, "Spirituality's Potential Relevance"; VanderWeele et al., "Attendance at Religious Services."

16. Hamdan et al., "Protective Factors and Suicidality."

17. Lee and Oh, "Validation of Reasons for Living"; Oquendo et al., "Protective Factors against Suicidal Behavior in Latinos"; Linehan et al., "Reasons for Staying Alive."

18. Pawlikowski et al., "Religious Service Attendance, Health Behaviors and Well-Being."

- positive emotions[19] and less negative emotionality[20]
- regulating one's emotional response or solving a problem[21]
- higher life satisfaction[22]
- less anger and alcohol use[23]
- learned competencies.[24]

Many people believe that what is important about church is social support. Social isolation is a problem[25] and getting support helps reduce mortality[26] and risk of suicide.[27] But there is a fair amount of research that has found that social support cannot explain all the benefits of church.[28] Social support in church attendance explains only about a quarter of the association between attendance and health.[29] People can get social support in a lot of places besides church.[30] The question remains: What in church protects against suicide?

Some of the protections in church happen organically. The four basic, universal dimensions of religion, the "Big Four Religious Dimensions,"[31] happen organically in most churches: believing,[32] bonding through

19. Chen and VanderWeele, "Religious Upbringing with Subsequent Health and Well-Being."

20. Morton et al., "Pathways from Religion to Health."

21. Marty et al., "Relationships among Dispositional Coping Strategies."

22. VanderWeele et al., "Reimagining Health"; Martín-María et al., "Impact of Subjective Well-Being."

23. Kim and VanderWeele, "Mediators of the Association."

24. Smith, "Theorizing Religious Effects."

25. Holt-Lunstad, "Potential Public Health Relevance of Social Isolation."

26. Holt-Lunstad et al., "Loneliness and Social Isolation as Risk Factors."

27. Brenner et al., "Suicidality and Veterans."

28. Edlund et al., "Religiosity and Decreased Risk of Substance Use"; Mason et al., "Suicidal Ideation."

29. VanderWeele et al., "Response."

30. Rasic et al., "Spirituality, Religion and Suicidal Behavior"; Rushing et al., "Relationship of Religious Involvement Indicators"; Wang et al., "Suicide Protective Factors in Outpatient Substance Abuse Patients."

31. Saroglou, "Believing, Bonding, Behaving, and Belonging."

32. Believing (cognitive) is holding a set of beliefs about transcendent entities, i.e., something larger and more important than me exists, which is meaning-making by aiming to find the truth (Saroglou, "Believing, Bonding, Behaving, and Belonging," 1323).

rituals,[33] behaving morally,[34] and belonging.[35] We have found aspects of these Big Four in our studies of churches. Churches organically provide life-affirming beliefs that encourage choosing life; they provide communal rituals that bond people to God, to life-affirming beliefs, and to each other; and they provide a safe community to which to belong and through which to develop a spiritual identity. But there is more than that which occurs in churches. Our research suggests that people who go to church feel compelled by their core Christian identity to "live a life of faith together" within a church that fosters spiritual "relational growing."[36] Whereas non-religious group members in our study[37] valued caring, supportive relationships, religious group members in our study valued the caring, supportive relationships focused on open, non-superficial, vulnerable spiritual sharing, which they viewed as vital to their faith. For example, one respondent said,

> If I am going to pick [my work group or ultimate Frisbee group] or [my church groups] to have an actual deep connection with, it's for sure going to be the faith-based groups, because we all just get more vulnerable and share things with each other and we listen to each other.[38]

People who go to church want to grow in their faith and adhere to "the same morals and similar ethic."[39] They want the help of other Christians to live out a life of faith.[40] Church attendance helps religious individuals with ways to manage their suicidal thoughts, by "shaping a person's beliefs," in

33. Bonding (emotional) is having self-transcendent, emotional experiences like awe through ritual that binds one to others and to a deeper reality that transcends the everyday reality and the self. (Awe facilitates spiritual behavior intentions. "Hope is a self-transcendent emotion" [Saroglou, "Believing, Bonding, Behaving, and Belonging," 1326].)

34. Behaving (moral) is subscribing to certain moral norms as defined *from a religious perspective*, and exerting self-control to behave in accordance with these norms and to achieve irreproachable virtue (Saroglou, "Believing, Bonding, Behaving, and Belonging," 1326).

35. Belonging (social identity) is identifying and affiliating with a certain community or tradition resulting in a social identity (Saroglou, "Believing, Bonding, Behaving, and Belonging," 1327).

36. Mason et al., "Unique Experiences in Religious Groups," 614, 619.

37. Mason et al., "Unique Experiences in Religious Groups."

38. Mason et al., "Unique Experiences in Religious Groups," 615.

39. Mason et al., "Unique Experiences in Religious Groups," 619.

40. Thoits, "Mechanisms Linking Social Ties and Support."

fostering "moral and religious objections to suicide"[41] and reasons to live in the context of a supportive community.

But there is more. We have found five factors in faith communities that protect against suicide:[42]

1. *A safe, connected community*, where the community engages in four activities (a) raising awareness of suicide, (b) fostering a stigma-free community which allows the safe, confidential disclosure of suicidal thinking, because faith leaders or congregants disclose their own struggles, (c) fostering a community where congregants have a sense of belonging and mattering, and (d) developing a safe, connected culture as opposed to a program.

2. *Life-affirming teaching*. Respondents described the protection of teachings focused either on the value of each life or hope in the midst of suffering. Respondents said that these life-affirming beliefs communicated through preaching or teaching helped a faith community engage with faith traditions that protect against suicide.

3. *Personal*[43] *and communal spiritual factors*. Respondents described the power of prayer, reading sacred scriptures, and worship singing, both personally and communally, as protecting against suicide.

4. *A skilled, equipped community*. Respondents described bringing in outside resources to equip an entire faith community with a model of suicide intervention in order to increase the skill of faith leaders, lay leaders, and congregants in intervening with a suicidal person.

5. *A well-networked community*. Respondents described networking synergistically with local community resources like mental health providers. They viewed access to local resources as a crucial protection.

Churches provide three of these organically (1) a *safe, connected community* where congregants experience a sense of belonging and mattering, (2) *life-affirming teaching*, and (3) *personal and communal spiritual factors*. Because

---

41. Lawrence et al., "Religion and Suicide Risk," 11, 15.

42. Mason et al., "How Counselors Can Help."

43. While this book does not focus on personal spiritual practices, research suggests that people who engage with Scripture four or more days a week have more positive life outcomes. goTandem (https://www.gotandem.com/) can help, based on research by Pamela Caudill Ovwigho, PhD, Executive Director, Center for Bible Engagement (Ovwigho et al., "Private Spiritual Practices").

churches provide these protections organically, there is little investment required. However, three protections are suicide prevention specific and require an investment of effort: (1) *a safe, connected community,* a stigma-free community allowing for the safe confidential disclosure of suicidal thinking, because faith leaders or congregants disclose their own struggles; (2) *a skilled, equipped community,* equipped with a model of suicide intervention in order to increase the skill of faith leaders and congregants in helping a suicidal person; and (3) *a well-networked community* connected to local community resources. This book will explain how a church can implement all of these. Let's start with the importance of life-affirming teaching.

The Power of Life-Affirming Teaching: Reflecting Theologically to Prevent Suicide

The US suicide rate has increased annually since 1999,[44] except for a slight drop in 2019. (During a national crisis like a pandemic, the suicide rate tends to go down because people pull together.)[45] But that is just the tip of the iceberg. For every suicide death, many more Americans attempt suicide and even more think about it.[46] About eight million Americans per year think about suicide.[47] You may think, "These people are not in the church." But in one of our studies, about 11 percent of congregant respondents were thinking about suicide at the time of the study.[48] Churches have been devastated by the loss of their pastors to suicide.[49] Suicide happens inside the walls of the church. But how could a Christian become suicidal?

44. The number and proportion of Americans lost to suicide has steadily climbed from 29,199 in 1999 (10.5 deaths per 100,000 US population) to 47,511 in 2019 (14.5 per 100,000). See Centers for Disease Control and Prevention, "WISQARS."

45. Joiner et al., "On Buckeyes, Gators, Super Bowl Sunday, and the Miracle on Ice."

46. For every fourteen suicides per 100,000 people each year, approximately *500* people per 100,000 attempt suicide, and *3,000* people per 100,000 think about suicide (Kessler et al., "Trends in Suicide Ideation").

47. Draper, *National Best Practices.*

48. In a sample of 745 Jewish, Catholic, and Protestant congregants, 11.41 percent ($n = 85$) said they currently had thoughts of suicide (Mason et al., "Suicidal Ideation").

49. Inland Hills (Chino, California) Lead Pastor Andrew Stoecklein died by suicide on August 25, 2018. Pastor Jarrid Wilson died by suicide September 9, 2019. Pastor Steve Austin died by suicide June 5, 2021.

Diana Gruber has written about Christians throughout history who became depressed.[50] C.H. Spurgeon, the "Prince of Preachers,"[51] preached in 1866, "I am the subject of depressions of spirit so fearful that I hope none of you ever gets to such extremes of wretchedness as I go to."[52] Christians have also become suicidal. Edward J. Carnell (past president of Fuller Seminary) wrote, "One Friday afternoon . . . I emotionally exploded . . . even suicide took on a certain attractiveness."[53]

You might ask, how could this be? Christians can become suicidal for at least four reasons:

1. Christians are redeemed *and* fallen. We read in 1 John 1:8, "If we claim to be without sin, we deceive ourselves and the truth is not in us." Sin results in brokenness in our lives, which means that no Christian has it "all-together."

2. Satan is determined to destroy Christians. The Apostle Peter tells us: "Your enemy the devil prowls around like a roaring lion looking for someone to devour" (1 Pet 5:8). Satan's determination to harm us can add to the brokenness in our lives.

3. God doesn't protect Christians from suffering, and suffering is not a failure of faith. Jesus was "in anguish" (Luke 22:44). The Apostle Paul and Timothy were under such pressure that they "despaired of life itself" (2 Cor 1:8). Many people of faith suffered horrible deaths (Heb 11:37). Faith in God doesn't prevent suffering. The Apostle Paul tells us that all Christians are groaning. "Not only so, but we ourselves, who have the first fruits of the Spirit, groan inwardly as we wait eagerly for our adoption to sonship, the redemption of our bodies" (Rom 8:23). Psychologist Gay Hubbard has written that God doesn't conform to our expectations that he will prevent suffering. She writes,

   > Contrary to [the thinking that "He'll fix it so I won't have to live through it"], God refuses to play the magician's role, nor is God in the business of providing free placebos or heavenly strength aspirin. The idea that if we can only get our burdens to God He will make us instantly feel better is bitterly unfair misdirection to people in pain . . . this "fix-it" approach makes

50. Gruver, *Companions in the Darkness.*

51. Adcock, *Charles H. Spurgeon.*

52. Spurgeon, "Joy and Peace in Believing."

53. Carnell, *Christian Commitment,* 11.

> pain a measure of our distance from God. Indirectly, this idea
> encourages us to think, "If I hurt, I'm a long way from God. If I
> were close to Him, He would make the hurt go away." The God
> of all comfort . . . is an identity quite different . . . from the idea
> of God as the "Great Pain Reliever."[54]

A person of faith will likely suffer, and some might become suicidal. Pastor Amy Fondroy Eich, whom we will meet in the next chapter, is clear that many Christians believe that "If you pray enough and go to church enough and are active enough in your faith life, then you're not going to experience suicidal thinking."[55] Believing God will prevent suffering or suicidal thinking is the kind of theology that can prevent churches from understanding that some of their congregants may be thinking about suicide and can stop churches from helping them.

4. Christians suffer in Christian ways and un-Christian ways. One of the un-Christian ways Christians suffer is being angry at God for allowing suffering. Job's wife didn't expect to lose everything. She said to Job, "Are you still maintaining your integrity? Curse God and die!" (Job 2:9). Research shows that "Religion is associated with greater physical and mental health except . . . when religious people feel angry or punished by God or deserted by God."[56] Jonah was suicidal and angry at God when God didn't do what he wanted. We read in Jonah 4:1–3, 9:

> But to Jonah [God not destroying Ninevah] seemed very
> wrong, and he became angry. He prayed to the Lord, "Isn't this
> what I said, Lord, when I was still at home? That is what I tried
> to forestall by fleeing to Tarshish. I knew that you are a gra-
> cious and compassionate God, slow to anger and abounding
> in love, a God who relents from sending calamity. Now, Lord,
> take away my life, for it is better for me to die than to live." . . .
> But God said to Jonah, "Is it right for you to be angry about the
> plant?" "It is," he said. "And I'm so angry I wish I were dead."

God doesn't accommodate himself to Jonah's expectations or to our expectations that we will not suffer. Christians need a clear theology of suffering: Christians suffer, suffering is not evidence of a weak faith, and sometimes Christians think about suicide.

---

54. Hubbard, *More Than an Aspirin*, 91.

55. Mason, "Suicide Stigma in Christian Faith Communities," 7.

56. Koenig et al., *Handbook of Religion and Health*, 97.

Christians need to reflect on other theological beliefs about suicide, such as the belief that "A person who dies by suicide goes to hell." In all my interviews with clergy, one thing comes through clearly: no one condones suicide.[57] This moral view point is argued from several perspectives, including the perspective of the sanctity of life and the preservation of the natural course of life.[58] As Pastor Amy Fondroy Eich says, "Suicide is not what God wants."[59] Many[60] people feel that suicide is a violation of something deep in the human psyche,[61] something that is morally objectionable. Durkheim, a secular Jew, wrote, "common morality reproves [suicide]."[62] Dr. Joshua Rottman and his colleagues write, "Even self-described non-religious liberals consider suicide to be morally wrong."[63] One pastor said, "I don't think that choosing your own end . . . counts as fulfilling your purpose."[64] Her point is that suicide is not an appropriate choice. Even secular mental health professionals who tolerate diverse views will do what they can to prevent suicide.[65] For example, Dr. Thomas Joiner and his colleagues write,

> We do not believe that people who die by suicide are making informed, rational decisions to do so. We also strongly believe in the value in preventing something that causes so much suffering for those directly affected by suicidal thoughts as well as their loved ones.[66]

Whether suicide is called a "sin" or "a moral wrong" or "doesn't fulfill your purpose," the message is the same: "Choose life." Generally, people don't approve of suicide and tell others to please not do it.

However, what happens when a Christian dies by suicide? Christian theologies about suicide include beliefs that suicide is a sin and that

57. Mason et al., "Moral Deliberations."

58. Mason et al., "Moral Deliberations."

59. Author interview with Pastor Amy Fondroy Eich, February 21, 2021.

60. Some do not. For example, Fedden believes that suicide is amoral, "There is something very niggard, very middle-class, very non-conformist, in judging a life by its exodus" (Fedden, *Suicide*, 13).

61. Gesundheit believes Judaism considers suicide a sin (Gesundheit, "Suicide"). In Islam, Allah punishes suicide. See 4:29 in the Koran.

62. Durkheim, *Suicide*, 327.

63. Rottman et al., "Tainting the Soul," 223.

64. Mason, *Preventing Suicide.*

65. Szasz dissents. See Szasz, "Case against Suicide Prevention."

66. Joiner et al., *Interpersonal Theory of Suicide*, 168.

suicide is not a sin. Some like Martin Luther believe suicide is not a sin because the person who attempts or dies by suicide has diminished responsibility due to mental illness or demonic activity. For example, Luther said, "I don't share the opinion that suicides are certainly to be damned. My reason is that they do not wish to kill themselves but are overcome by the power of the devil."[67] One of our study participants agreed, "[Suicide] is not a matter of selfishness, it's not a matter of morality, it's about people being in, what feels like, unendurable pain."[68]

Augustine in the sixth century argued that suicide is a sin based on the sixth commandment (Exod 20:13: "You shall not murder"; see also Gen 9:6). Augustine argued, "The law, rightly interpreted, even prohibits suicide, where it says, 'You shall not kill.' This is proved especially by the omission of the words 'your neighbor.'"[69] If Christians believe that suicide is a sin, they argue that suicide is a sin based on the sanctity of life, that life is sacred and inviolable (Deut 32:39; Job 1:21; 1 Cor 6:19–20; Eph 5:29; Phil 1:20–26), that only God can take life, and that suicide goes against the principle of the preservation of the natural course of life. For example, John Calvin said, "Let us wait for the highest commander, who sent us into this world, to call us out of it."[70]

Most Christians who believe that suicide is a sin argue that it is a forgivable sin based on the verses that say the only unpardonable sin is blasphemy against the Holy Spirit (Matt 12:31) or the sin unto death (1 John 5:16), which does not clearly refer to suicide. They argue that even our righteousness is as filthy rags (Isa 64:6), that all sin requires Christ's righteousness and grace (Eph 2:8–9), that nothing can separate us from the love of God (Rom 8:38–39), that God deals with our sin not as we deserve (Ps 103:10), that Jesus is a friend of sinners (Luke 7:34), and that we will all die of unrepented of sins we didn't recognize as sin. Lewis Smedes adds, "But all of us commit sins that we are too spiritually cloddish to recognize for the sins they are. And we all die with sins not named and repented of."[71] Rev. Dr. Sherry Molock, co-pastor of Beloved Community Church, adds,

> There is nothing that separates us from the love of God, even your suicidal thoughts. I think there is nothing you can't be forgiven

67. Luther, "Table Talk," 29.

68. Unpublished interview from Mason et al., "How Counselors Can Help."

69. Augustine, *City of God*, I.20.

70. John Calvin, quoted in Watt, *Choosing Death*, 67–68.

71. Smedes, "Good Question."

> for. I think for people who say, "You don't get to repent," we don't
> know what God is doing in the last moments of someone's life.
> And I think within a Christian context, saying that you can't
> be forgiven for something is saying that Jesus died for nothing,
> that His love and grace is not sufficient—therefore there can't be
> something that's unpardonable.[72]

If suicide is forgivable, then the person who dies by suicide is not condemned to hell. While many Christians believe that suicide is a forgivable sin, the fear of hell must be replaced by reasons to live, a theology of life. Dr. Melinda Moore (from ch. 7) tells about the rising suicide rates among young African American men.[73] She tells about Jerry and Elsi Weyrauch[74] talking with Dr. David Satcher, the surgeon general, about the rise in suicide rates in this group. Dr. Satcher concluded that the taboo around suicide in the Black church had changed, and this change was no longer preventing suicide. Because many youths no longer believed that suicide damns a person to hell, suicide was no longer held in check.

In the place of this theology, Christians need to offer a theology of life. Christians must answer the questions, "What is a good life?"; "What makes life worth living?"; "How do Christians build lives worth living?"; "Why stay alive in the midst of challenging circumstances?"; "Why should a person with diminished functioning stay alive?"; "What should [a suicidal person] do if he loses the good life?"; "What are the reasons to keep living when someone is in the midst of painful circumstances?"[75] In John 10:10, we read Jesus' words, "I have come that they may have life, and have it to the full." As Christians, we need to reflect on how to help suicidal Christians in our churches live this verse out. A study participant said, "We [in the church] don't quite grasp why people who are really struggling in life should live."[76] Irish Catholic Bishops published a pastoral letter on "Life is for living" to highlight a theology of life.[77] Christians need to reflect theologically on suffering, suicide, and "Why live?"

---

72. Unpublished interview from Mason et al., "How Counselors Can Help."

73. Coleman et al., *Ring the Alarm*.

74. Jerry and Elsi Weyrauch founded SPANUSA after losing their daughter Terri Ann to suicide: https://www.span-ga.org/history.

75. Gibson and Mason, *Preaching Hope in Darkness*, 11.

76. Unpublished interview from Mason et al., "How Counselors Can Help."

77. Irish Catholic Bishops, "Life Is for Living."

Some Definitions

Before we finish this chapter, we need to define what we are talking about. Suicide is a death caused by self-inflicted injuries with some intent to die. A suicide attempt is a self-inflicted, nonfatal injury with some evidence of intent to die. Suicidal ideation or thinking is any thoughts or mental images of suicide or of intent to take one's life. Suicidal behaviors capture the broad spectrum of suicidal thinking and behaviors. People who have lost a loved one to suicide will be called survivors of suicide loss. Survivors have asked me to say "die by suicide" instead of "commit suicide" because suicide is not a crime. I will quote study participants who say "commit suicide," but I will say "die by suicide" out of respect for survivors of suicide loss.

The Three Phases: Prevention, Intervention, and Postvention

What has struck me most in all my research is that churches contribute to suicide prevention very uniquely because they engage suicide across all three phases. As a psychologist, I engage suicide primarily in the intervention phase. Churches are unique in that they help prevent suicide across all three phases. In this chapter, we started digging the foundation of prevention by reflecting on how a church prevents suicide and by reflecting theologically on suffering, on a theology of suicide, and a theology of life.

Because suicide prevention is a broad task, there is room for a lot of people getting involved. Anyone in a church can have a role in suicide prevention in a church. Consider getting involved. This book will show you how. In the next chapter, we will continue digging the foundation of prevention by pouring the foundation of a safe, connected church.

Discussion Questions

1. A book on suicide prevention can be difficult. How will you take care of yourself as you read?

2. Why do you think that rates of suicide are lower among those who attend church regularly?

3. Why do you think Christians can be suicidal?

4. Why do you think Christians should stay alive even when life is difficult for them?

Take Stock of Your Church

1. Which of the three phases are already in place in your church?

2. Which of the three phases do you think is most important? Prevention? Intervention? Postvention? If you are building a suicide prevention culture in your church, with which phase would you start? How would you get started?

3. What does your church believe about suffering, suicide, and why people should stay alive in the midst of their suffering?

Resources

Gibson, Scott, and Karen Mason. *Preaching Hope in Darkness: Help for Pastors in Addressing Suicide from the Pulpit.* Bellingham: Lexham, 2020.

Mason, Karen. *Preventing Suicide: A Handbook for Pastors, Chaplains and Pastoral Counselors.* Downers Grove: InterVarsity, 2014.

988 Suicide & Crisis Lifeline. https://988lifeline.org/

CHAPTER 2

Essential Element 1:
A Safe, Connected Church

If you do away with the yoke of oppression,
with the pointing finger and malicious talk, . . .
then your light will rise in the darkness,
and your night will become like the noonday. (Isa 58:9–10)

Love each other as I have loved you. (John 15:12)

Who comforts us in all our troubles so that we can comfort those
in any trouble with the comfort we ourselves receive from God.
. . . Our conscience testifies that we have conducted ourselves . . .
especially in our relations with you, with integrity and godly sin-
cerity. (2 Cor 1:4, 12)

Pastor Amy Fondroy Eich attributes her openness to discussing suicide
to her experience of how her parents talked about a neighbor who died
of suicide. Amy remembers, "I could tell that my parents cared about the
family. That gave me permission to understand that suicide is something
tragic that happens." As an adult, after her parents had died, she found
a note in her dad's dresser. It was from the pastor who preached at the
neighbor's funeral, who wrote to her parents thanking them for their kind
words with a copy of the sermon. Amy says, "I was surprised how openly
the pastor talked about how the man died because of the weight of his
struggle. Now we would say struggle with mental health." When the wife
and kids moved away, Amy's parents agreed to continue to put flowers on
the grave site. The family stayed in touch over the years. This experience
shaped her openness to talking about suicide in church.

Pastor Amy wants to help people have open conversations about
subjects that aren't comfortable, like suicide, so that people in the church

don't feel they have to bring "their shiny pretty selves" to church. She wants churches to be able to say "all of you is welcome." She is convinced that God doesn't want people to be in a place where they feel so alone because they can't talk about suicide, even though she knows that takes courage. She says, "It takes people being bold and finding ways to start conversations."[1]

A safe, connected church is the next step in pouring the foundation for suicide prevention in a church. The foundation involves building a church where there is awareness about suicide, where a stigma-free community allows the safe confidential disclosure of suicidal thinking, because pastors and congregants disclose their own struggles with either mental health conditions or suicidal behaviors, and where congregants gain a sense of belonging and mattering (e.g., "I matter to this church"). Let's continue pouring this foundation by looking at the problem of stigma.

Why Is Stigma a Problem?

Heart attacks used to be blanketed in stigma.[2] When President Eisenhower suffered his first heart attack in 1955, the scientific community did not understand what caused heart attacks so people avoided talking about them. Cancer used to be called "the C-word." Pastor Amy says, "People used to not talk about cancer. Now there is a lot of conversation around cancer prevention screening." Suicide is far more stigmatized than a feared illness like cancer or COVID-19. A teen said, "I don't know a single person who has COVID or died of COVID, but I know kids who have died of suicide or drug overdose and there is not nearly the conversation around that." Pastor Amy yearns for more conversation about suicide prevention. Pastor Amy says, "I hope for a time when the same can be true about suicide, [when] people can know the word suicide, people can know there are resources available to help people through times of suicidal thinking." One of our pastor study participants shared this story:

> [In] my second year at the seminary, a fourth year student died by
> suicide. I was editor of the campus newspaper at the time. I went

1. Author interview with Pastor Amy Fondroy Eich, February 21, 2021. Pastor Amy Fondroy Eich is an ordained pastor in the Evangelical Lutheran Church in America. She has been a Soul Shop trainer. Soul Shop is a faith-based suicide prevention program.

2. Story shared by Robert Freedman, MD, when the Suicide Prevention Coalition of Colorado recognized his schizophrenia research as a vital contribution to suicide prevention. Story from Gibson and Mason, *Preaching Hope in Darkness*, 54.

> to the seminary president and I said, "As tragic as this is, I think this is an opportunity for us to talk about [suicide], not only to be real and transparent as a faith community here, but also for future pastors, how do we address this in the future?" He looked at me squarely in the eye and pointed his finger and said, "We will not talk about this. This is not something we discuss here."[3]

Stigma about suicide causes many problems, but the main one is that suicidal congregants may not reach out for help. Even though a fair number of people in a congregation might be suicidal,[4] pastors say that only about one or two suicidal people reach out to them for help each year.[5] Suicidal congregants may not reach out for help because stigma gets in the way.[6] Former Pastor Fe Anam Avis (from ch. 8) writes, "The subject [of suicide] is so frightening that the person who dies by suicide does not feel safe talking about it until he or she is dead. By that time, conversation is no longer a possibility."[7]

Not reaching out for help means that stigma significantly lessens a suicidal person's sense of community, which is *very* important to preventing suicide. Stigma can prevent suicidal people from feeling connected to their church. One of our study participants said that stigma means "I have to deal with this by myself, to myself."[8] Stigma can amplify a sense of loneliness and isolation. A suicidal congregant might decide, "My death will be worth more than my life to family, friends."[9] Pastor Amy adds,

> All stigmas can increase risk because it closes conversation or increases isolation. Whether it's someone feeling ashamed about "I don't have a good enough faith and that must be why I'm feeling

3. Unpublished interview from Mason et al., "How Counselors Can Help."

4. Former Pastor Fe Anam Avis estimates that on average, about thirty adults and additional adolescents in a congregation of five hundred are thinking about their own suicide on any given Sunday (Avis, *Second Day*, 112). We found in a sample of 745 Catholic, Jewish, and Protestant congregants that 11.41 percent ($n = 85$) reported having current thoughts of suicide (Mason et al., "Suicidal Ideation").

5. Clergy report being contacted on average by at least one suicidal individual per year, with an average of two contacts per year (Mason et al., "Clergy as Suicide Prevention Gatekeepers").

6. In a sample of 801 Catholic, Jewish, and Protestant clergy, the barriers to referral of suicidal people cited most frequently by clergy were finances (49 percent) and stigma (41 percent) (Mason et al., "Clergy as Suicide Prevention Gatekeepers").

7. Avis, *Second Day*, 11.

8. Mason, "Suicide Stigma in Christian Faith Communities."

9. Joiner et al., *Interpersonal Theory of Suicide*, 6.

> this way, so how can I reach out to someone?" or, "How could I be thinking about doing this to myself? I know this would be tragic for my family." Anything that shuts down the conversation or increases isolation increases the likelihood of someone dying of suicide.

Stigma is a problem because stigma is associated with increased suicidal thinking. One study found that college students who believed they shouldn't seek help for their mental health because people hold negative views of those seeking mental health treatment have increased risk of suicidal thoughts and suicide planning and attempts.[10] Stigma is associated with increased suicide risk.

What Do We Know about Stigma?

Social support is vital to physical health[11] and to psychological well-being.[12] Many people find social support in churches. Robert Putnam wrote that "Faith communities in which people worship together are arguably the single most important repository of social capital in America."[13] Jackson Carroll agrees, "Christians understand congregations to be a primary mode—arguably the primary mode—through which the Christian gospel is organizationally embodied and made visible."[14] The church is the body of Christ (1 Cor 12). Fe puts it this way:

> Our presence as a sacramental expression of the love of God can be decisive! When we understand that we are God's hands, every encounter is potentially lifesaving. When this attitude is carried in the soul of a community, hospitality is elevated from the status of "friendliness" to the "touch of life." We offer God's love as a holy wonder.[15]

---

10. Goodwill and Zhu, "Association between Perceived Public Stigma."

11. A meta-analysis of 148 studies comprising more than 308,000 people found that participants with stronger social relationships were 50 percent more likely to survive over the studies' given periods than those with weaker connections (Holt-Lunstad et al., "Social Relationships and Mortality Risk").

12. Moak and Agrawal, "Perceived Interpersonal Social Support and Physical and Mental Health."

13. Putnam, *Bowling Alone*, 66.

14. Carroll, *God's Potters*, 11.

15. Avis, *Second Day*, 110.

But churches are not perfect. Churches can have stigma about suicide. Nine Christian faith leaders and congregants described suicide stigma this way.[16] Being touched by suicide in some way is "a blemish" that makes others pull away. Some of the stigma is internal, some is interpersonal, and some is theological. Suicidal people worry they are "deficient" and project their internal "deep shame" onto others; they put on "a façade" of "having it all together," because they believe suicidal thinking is a failure of their faith, and suffer in secret silence as long as possible. If suicide becomes public, people touched by suicide might be shunned. Other congregants may fear that "if [suicide] can happen to your family, then it could happen to my family. Therefore, I will do everything possible to figure out how you are different from me." Stigma is based in erroneous theological beliefs, like "only weak Christians become suicidal." Because churches don't talk about suicide, people might "fill in that blank with old and often negative beliefs."

How does stigma get started in churches? Religions have always had norms that shouldn't be broken.[17] Breaking a norm generates a sense of moral disgust.[18] Disgust is a feeling of strong distaste or repulsion. For example, we might feel moral disgust for a sex offender who transgresses a sexual norm. Disgust is often associated with a feeling that something pure has been violated. For example, a vegetarian might feel disgust after seeing another person eat meat because they have a view of vegetarianism as the pure state of being. When this pure state of being is violated, the vegetarian feels disgust.

Disgust is very automatic. We might feel disgust without being conscious of it. Dr. Jonathan Haidt believes that our judgments about morality are instantaneous, a "flash of insight" that we experience rapidly outside of consciousness.[19] That process can be slowed down. Dr. Joshua Rottman will show us how.

Rottman, a moral psychologist, has found that disgust appears to be uniquely associated with purity judgments. He found that suicide generates a feeling of disgust because suicide is considered a moral violation that taints or degrades the soul and makes it "impure."[20] Rottman goes on to explain

---

16. Mason, "Suicide Stigma in Christian Faith Communities."

17. Saroglou, "Believing, Bonding, Behaving, and Belonging," 1327.

18. Tybur et al., "Disgust."

19. Haidt and Joseph, "Intuitive Ethics." See also Haidt, "Emotional Dog and Its Rational Tail."

20. Rottman et al., "Tainting the Soul," 218.

that "impure" people tend to be cast out of groups and marginalized through stigma. Impure people are stigmatized as less trustworthy, less friendly, less smart. He says that we tend to dehumanize stigmatized people and not afford them the same kind of moral concern that others get. There is less moral responsibility that we feel toward protecting their rights.

A suicidal person picks up on the disgust of others. Suicide prevention consultant Fe Anam Avis writes, "When a subject is shameful in a culture, a change of subject, a knitted brow, a looking away is a powerful conveyer of the message."[21] These non-verbal messages get internalized by the suicidal person. Doris Lessing writes that "the dance between disgust and shame takes place."[22] The suicidal person may feel "deep shame"[23] and may not reach out for help, or the church may avoid the suicidal person or not give them as much help as they need. The disgust "motivates avoidance of social relationships with norm-violating individuals."[24] The result is social distancing at a time when a suicidal person most needs to be supported by their church. "The greatest problem for someone who is wrestling with suicide is finding someone to talk to."[25] Pastor Rachel writes about not reaching out: "I used to be afraid of anyone finding out that I had tried to kill myself. I didn't want anyone to think I was crazy. I didn't want to be dismissed."[26] People who have lost a loved one to suicide can experience the same shame and social distance[27] at a time when they need social support.

How Do We Build a Safe Church Community?

So what should churches do about stigma to build a safe community where suicidal people can reach out for help and get the support they need? A lot of research has shown that people can tolerate pain better when they feel the empathy of others.[28] How do we pour a foundation of safety and connectedness to prevent suicide? The first step is to recognize

21. Avis, *Second Day*, 38.

22. Lessing, *Golden Notebook*.

23. Mason, "Suicide Stigma in Christian Faith Communities."

24. Tybur et al., "Microbes, Mating, and Morality," 107.

25. Avis, *Second Day*, 21.

26. Keefe, *Lifesaving Church*, 49.

27. Kucukalic and Kucukalic, "Stigma and Suicide."

28. Duschek et al., "Dispositional Empathy"; Goldstein et al., "Brain-to-Brain Coupling."

that as Pastor Jim Liske has said, "All of our churches have people in them who are struggling [with mental health]. . . . When you are suffering from mental illness, it is not sin. Let's get over that one."[29] Suicidal people are also in the church.[30] Even Christians of great faith like Dr. Edward Carnell have struggled with suicidal thinking.

Another aspect of building a safe community is to focus on suicide as harm. Rottman has found that viewing suicide as tainting your soul is a sticky stigma that is hard to get rid of. Harm violations are easier to change.[31] Harm violations are "anything that is going to negatively impact others or going to cause suffering."[32] Punching someone in the nose is an example of a harm violation. Harm violations carry less stigma and are easier to change. Instead of looking at suicide as tainting a soul, the church needs to see the harm, the harm to the suicidal person and the harm to loss survivors. Seeing the harm may lead to less stigma. Suicidal people are already suffering but the lack of care the church shows them intensifies their suffering. Rottman says,

> To the extent that stigma is related to ideas about purity and feelings of disgust, we're going to distance ourselves not only from people who attempt or commit suicide but we're going to distance ourselves from the concept, from talking about suicide, by having this purity framework. . . . Whereas with harm, people are much more likely to engage with the idea. . . . It's easier for people to have good discourse about something in the domain of harm, when it's framed as a harm-based issue.

We need to see that the suicidal congregant suffers in their suicidal thinking and loss survivors suffer in their grief. Stigma that keeps the church from showing them care intensifies their suffering. The church's avoidance of them harms them. These are suffering people who deserve the church's love and ministry. The stigma of suicide needs to be challenged with God's admonition that we love one another, including people touched by suicide. In 1 Corinthians 12:24–26, we read,

> But God has put the body together, giving greater honor to the parts that lacked it, so that there should be no division in the body,

29. Unpublished interview from Mason et al., "How Counselors Can Help."

30. Mason et al., "Suicidal Ideation."

31. Rottman and Young, "Specks of Dirt and Tons of Pain."

32. Rottman, from interview with author.

> but that its parts should have equal concern for each other. If one
> part suffers, every part suffers with it.

Moral convictions about suicide need to be balanced with love. Moral convictions are important because people join churches to learn about norms that help them build lives worth living; they join churches in order to be formed spiritually into a particular set of beliefs and to be held to these beliefs through positive peer influence.[33] This applies to beliefs about suicide. Christians can have moral convictions about suicide, but those convictions must be balanced with love. How do we do this? We do this by remembering that suicide is not just a moral issue; it is also about psychological suffering. A suicidal Christian is experiencing anguish and misery. Cornelius Plantinga argues, "Sin makes us guilty while disease makes us miserable. We thus need grace for our sin but mercy and healing for our disease."[34] Suicidal Christians are important people in our congregations. Christians value the lives of unborn children and ought also to value the life of a suicidal Christian. Lewis Smedes adds,

> As Christians, we should worry less about whether Christians who
> have killed themselves go to heaven, and worry more about how
> we can help people like them find hope and joy in living. Our most
> urgent problem is not the morality of suicide but the spiritual and
> mental despair that drags people down to it.[35]

In one of our studies, we found that pastors always focus on pastoral care before they focus on theology. One of the most important findings of the study was "[pastors'] profound concern for the well-being of suffering individuals and the clear priority of pastoral care over sharing the moral stance of their faith tradition."[36] The church needs to focus on the suffering of people touched by suicide and think about how to minister to them. With this focus, we can do what one study participant called "actively remove the stigma."[37]

In order to help a church have difficult conversations about the stigma of suicide, the church needs to develop some basic skills. Consultant Fe

---

33. Mason et al., "Unique Experiences in Religious Groups," 620.

34. Plantinga, *Not the Way*, 20, 64.

35. Smedes, "Good Question."

36. Mason et al., "Moral Deliberations," 345.

37. Unpublished interview from Mason et al., "How Counselors Can Help."

says, "The problems in churches are many, but the solutions are few."[38] He recommends helping churches develop the basic abilities of being quick to listen and slow to speak. Dr. Amy L. Eva suggests these two skills[39] (with my examples of how these skills apply to conversations about suicide):

1. *Awareness of any biases.* Ask, "What are the stories you tell yourself about suicide? What are your implicit biases, values, and beliefs about suicide?" People need to gain an awareness of their prejudices about suicide and suicidal people.

2. *Navigating strong emotions and managing them.* Ask, "How do you keep your calm during discussions about suicide? How will you navigate your emotions in a fueled conversation?" Eva advises teaching how to notice your reactions, take a deep breath and take the time to decide how to respond. Doing so helps us to regulate our emotions enough to increase empathy and perspective-taking.

Pastor Amy points out that learning to have these conversations will directly benefit the suicidal person who needs someone to talk to. She says,

> It's a relief for someone to talk about suicide. The same is true about divorce or financial struggles or not getting along well with their kids, that their kids are struggling in school. Learning how to talk about subjects that we're not comfortable with helps [everyone in church].

In these discussions, address suicide stigma explicitly. Naming suicide delays the process of stigma being automatically and unconsciously triggered. I have seen churches challenge stigma in one of three ways. The first way normalizes suicide, suggesting that suicide is a common human experience. The second way normalizes mental health conditions, suggesting that suicide is related to the common human experience of having a mental health condition. The third way combines the approaches.

1. *Normalize suicide.* Fe says that suicidal thinking is extremely common. He estimates that on average, about thirty adults and additional adolescents in a congregation of five hundred are thinking about their own suicide on any given Sunday.[40] In one of our studies, we found 11 percent of congregants who responded to our survey had current

---

38. Author interview with Fe Anam Avis, February 16, 2021.
39. Eva and Thayer, "Mindful Teacher."
40. Avis, *Second Day*, 112.

thoughts of suicide.[41] In another, a study participant said, "There is a lot of collective arrogance that's hidden underneath this assumption that not all people . . . can have the thought about whether it's worth it to continue [life]."[42] The fact that suicide is a part of the human experience means that the body of Christ will include suicidal Christians.

2. *Normalize mental health conditions.* One in five Americans has a mental health condition and a range of treatments that work exists for most mental health conditions.[43] But nearly two-thirds of all people with diagnosable mental disorders do not seek treatment. The "most formidable obstacle to future progress in the arena of mental illness and health is stigma."[44] Globally, for nearly three decades, depressive disorders continue to be one of the leading causes of non-fatal health loss.[45] The fact that mental health conditions are a part of the human experience means that churches have congregants with mental health conditions.

3. *Combine the approaches.* Pastor Talitha (from ch. 4) focuses on both. She said, "Congregational ministry is just messy by its definition, so to separate those two things doesn't make any sense to me."[46]

See Appendix A at the end of this chapter for an outline for how to lead a civil conversation about suicide. These are the same skills that would be needed in a church to talk about any difficult issue, including racism.

How to Build Transparent Authenticity

The final task of building a safe community is to normalize reaching out for help. Fe Anam Avis writes,

> Given the prevalence of suicidal thinking in a typical congregation, and given the fact that it will be an issue over the life span of nearly everyone, it makes sense that it be addressed sacramentally. If we circumscribe marriage, ordination, confirmation, and

41. Mason et al., "Suicidal Ideation."

42. Unpublished interview from Mason et al., "How Counselors Can Help."

43. US Department of Health and Human Services, *Mental Health.*

44. US Department of Health and Human Services, *Mental Health.*

45. Global Health Metrics, "Systematic Analysis for the Global Burden of Disease Study."

46. Mason et al., "How Counselors Can Help."

baptism with vows, doesn't it make sense that we call members to take a vow that they will disclose suicidal thinking when it occurs in their lives, especially since life and death are on the line? This is a vow that could be remembered and recalled at critical junctures.[47]

Pastor Amy suggests: "In trainings, ask people to make a commitment to reach out for help." In Soul Shop's commitment to life liturgy, participants write down the names of three people they vow to tell if they are thinking about suicide. One of my heroes in the Bible is Blind Bartimaeus (Mark 10:46–52). Bartimaeus reached out for help. Even though his community tried to silence him, he shouted, "Jesus, Son of David, have mercy on me!" He reached out and Jesus healed him. May we all be like Blind Bartimaeus.

People are more likely to reach out for help when the church fosters a culture of transparent authenticity where no one needs to present "their shiny pretty selves" at church (says Pastor Amy), or where they can present "warts and all" (says Pastor Talitha from ch. 4). One way churches do this is to ask a person with lived experience with suicide to tell their story. This is called the "contact method," which includes education plus contact with a person with experience.[48] A study participant said that everything in church needs to give "permission to be real and authentic."[49] The goal is for the pastor or a congregant to share about their own struggles with either mental health or suicide in order to foster an honest transparency.[50] A pastor in one of our studies said,

> I almost committed suicide when I was twenty-one years old, and I am not shy about sharing that experience. I have been transparent, and others have been transparent in the hope that if that's where someone is, that they would feel comfortable bringing it up thinking, "I'm not the only one," or "They've been there, and they have talked about it."[51]

---

47. Avis, *Second Day*, 113.

48. Corrigan, "Mental Health Stigma as Social Attribution"; Corrigan et al., "Familiarity with and Social Distance"; Corrigan et al., "Prejudice, Social Distance, and Familiarity."

49. Unpublished interview from Mason et al., "How Counselors Can Help."

50. Mason et al., "How Counselors Can Help."

51. Unpublished interview from Mason et al., "How Counselors Can Help."

Another pastor invites pastors to share their own experience with depression "So people can see we can talk about this."[52] A congregant in one of our studies described this transparency: "People feel like they don't have to hide. The culture doesn't ask them to put on a happy face. Leaders are modeling transparency and admitting they've got their own issues."[53] Another participant concurred, "[Churches] set a culture where it's okay to struggle, and be open and authentic about that. . . . So there is not this sort of projection that we're all perfect."[54] One participant emphasized that this culture is fostered intentionally through vulnerable sharing,

> The greatest obstacle is courage just to be that first person that raises their hand and says, "I have anxiety or I have depression and I am thinking of suicide." . . . Whether we like it or not, the pastor is the rock star of the concert, and the more they share, the more permission is given to be honest about suicidal ideation and making sure that we talk about it.[55]

Many study participants have emphasized the importance of the pastor's vulnerability.[56] Pastor Amy lays out the theology for this authentic transparency in a church:

> Church is there because of our broken selves. Humans need places where we can bring our brokenness. . . . Church is a place where all of you is welcome. God created you and that's why you're welcome, and we're in a world that is full of brokenness and God is here to hold that brokenness.

Pastor Amy adds that this process requires boldness: "It takes people being bold and finding ways to start conversations."

Sharing Your Experience with Suicide

When sharing your story, Pastor Talitha cautions to "not do therapy from the pulpit. A good therapist can help you figure out how not to bring your baggage" to the telling of your story. She did therapy with a psychologist for six years, which helped her be a better minister. Having intentionality

52. Unpublished interview from Mason et al., "How Counselors Can Help."

53. Unpublished interview from Mason et al., "How Counselors Can Help."

54. Unpublished interview from Mason et al., "How Counselors Can Help."

55. Mason et al., "How Counselors Can Help."

56. Unpublished interview from Mason et al., "How Counselors Can Help."

over a long period of time helped her "sort out the real issues." As a result, she found "I have more insight." When she decided to include her family's story of suicide in a sermon on Jesus' healing of a man with an unclean spirit, the only way she gave herself permission to do that was by knowing that her family would not hear the sermon. (She was serving a church across the country and the services weren't recorded or aired.) Moreover, she wasn't preaching the sermon to get back at her family, nor was she using preaching to do her therapy from the pulpit. She had enough distance from her story. "Yes, stories are important, but you've got to do your homework ahead of time, so that you are not doing therapy from the pulpit *ever*." She made clear in her sermon that sharing her story was not to bring attention to her but to bring attention to mental health issues. Appendix B at the end of the chapter includes some suggestions for those who might want to share their story.

Soul Shop Can Help

One way that churches have fostered a safe place where suicidal congregants can reach out is through a Soul Shop training.[57] Pastor Amy describes "Soul Shop for Leaders" as a standardized six-hour training which raises awareness of suicide in congregations and equips congregants to recognize the signs of suicide and how to intervene.[58] Soul Shop is a skills-based training. Soul Shop will also help the church develop a list of community resources so that "the whole community is working together" to keep people safe.[59] Networking is important because Soul Shop takes the perspective that mental health is not the sole driver of suicidal desperation; the more important driver is that a suicidal person's life is not working for them. A suicidal person needs resources. Finally, Soul Shop will help your church develop a church culture "where people are protected from suicide," which includes a discussion about theology.[60] Soul Shop also offers programs for youth leaders and campus ministry leaders, where contagion is discussed.

As you begin the process of pouring the foundation for suicide prevention, it is important to understand that not everyone in the church will get on board with suicide prevention. Suicide prevention consultant Fe

---

57. See the web page: https://www.soulshopmovement.org/ourworkshops.

58. Unpublished interview from Mason et al., "How Counselors Can Help."

59. Unpublished interview from Mason et al., "How Counselors Can Help."

60. Unpublished interview from Mason et al., "How Counselors Can Help."

says, "Any man who takes a journey must forgive those who do not go with him or else he never begins."[61] Part of our task is to identify people who are willing to take this journey and forgive those who don't. In the next chapter, we will continue to pour the foundation for suicide prevention through a life-affirming church.

Discussion Questions

1. How have you experienced stigma in society or in church?

2. How is suicide stigmatized?

3. How have you navigated "sticky" stigmas around other issues like HIV/AIDS?

4. How would you navigate the "sticky" stigma of suicide?

5. How does a church perpetuate or challenge stigma?

Take Stock of Your Church

1. Are there ways that people are excluded from your church life?[62]

2. In what ways does stigma of suicide need to be addressed in your church community?

3. Can your church talk about difficult topics?

4. What core relational skills does your church need to develop in order to have a civil discourse and challenge stigma?

5. How would you challenge suicide stigma in your church?

Resources

The Evangelical Lutheran Church in America's statement on suicide prevention. https://www.elca.org/Faith/Faith-and-Society/Social-Messages/Suicide-Prevention
988 Suicide & Crisis Lifeline. https://988lifeline.org/
Soul Shop faith-based suicide prevention training. https://www.soulshopmovement.org/

61. Avis, *Second Day*, 80.
62. Avis, *Second Day*, 113–14.

CHAPTER 3

Essential Element 2: A Life-Affirming Church

Return to your fortress, you prisoners of hope; even now I announce that I will restore twice as much to you. (Zech 9:12)

So the Twelve gathered all the disciples together and said, "It would not be right for us to neglect the ministry of the word of God in order to wait on tables." (Acts 6:2)

We must pay the most careful attention, therefore, to what we have heard, so that we do not drift away. (Heb 2:1)

A skilled homiletician, Rev. Dr. Scott M. Gibson tells his story.

My aunt died by suicide. And it was really in many ways a big family secret. As suicide is, it sneaks up on people and is an incredible shock and many people don't know how to handle it and our family didn't know how to handle it. Even though we know she died, it was not really talked about, the way in which she died. The coffin sitting in the middle of the room was almost like an elephant to us because really we didn't address that issue at all. She suffered from depression. We all knew that. She struggled from separation from her long-time marriage. She felt a failure. Her kids really struggled with how to help her. She lived alone, was dealing with some health issues. But mainly the depression was the illness that crushed her, which eventually led her to take an overdose and die by suicide. Somebody asks, "Was that intentional?" Well, we really think it was intentional, because she wanted to escape the pain she was suffering. I remember going to the funeral. The minister who was officiating knew that my family didn't come from any type of Christian background. But for some reason, they were associated with the Presbyterian church. They really never darkened the doors of a Presbyterian church building. The Presbyterian pastor and I were chatting. And I was a young high school student who sensed that God was leading me into the ministry. And I never forget his words he said to me, "This family really has problems." And as a young eighteen year old, I really didn't know how to handle that. I knew my family had trouble. But the way in which they dealt with trouble was laying there in the casket before us. That was my first exposure to somebody dying by suicide and having to deal with it. And basically, we all dealt with it privately. It was stuffed down inside. It really wasn't until I became a pastor and dealt with people who had suicidal ideation or different kinds of threats to one's life through suicide that I started to think more about it. I still felt very much at a loss for how to address it in the church.

The circumstances of the death and the guilt from it and the pain were never really dealt with. There was blame, unarticulated blame, placed on my uncle who separated from my aunt. There was a lot of blame on him and how that had put her in a place, especially as a woman not having resources. She was living in an apartment. She bore a financial burden. I wouldn't have realized it back then when I was eighteen years old, but now I do. I can see the only way she could escape that was to escape it by suicide. We don't realize the layers of complication that are present in somebody's life and mind, that tips them toward attempt or to go through a suicide. My family has never talked about it since. It is stuffed. When I talk to my siblings, they don't want to talk about it, face the reality of what had happened. Yet it is so clear as to what happened. But it's better left pushed down. It's probably been forty-five years since her death. Even now, it's something that is an embarrassment for some folks, that that's how she died. At family reunions, there is no talk about her death and the way in which she died.

A suicide in my extended family happened a few years ago. A military officer, who grew up in a strict Catholic family, murdered his wife and his two children. He called his mother to tell her he loved her and "I've had it." He then killed himself. His devoted Catholic commitments didn't prevent him from killing his family and himself. There must have been some kind of mental illness that overtook him that prevented him from being moored by his faith commitments. Instead, he was adrift and saw that as the only solution. His mother is a devoted Catholic. This public suicide "rocked her world." Because of the diminishment of the Catholic Church and the problem with priests, getting them assigned, nobody came to minister to her. I was the only minister who came to visit her. Even her other son, he left the Catholic Church and has been going to a Baptist church, and even the Baptist pastor didn't come.

> The daughter had left the Catholic Church and goes to a Christian
> Missionary Alliance church, and that pastor didn't come. I think
> that there is that shock factor, stigma, and it was easy for them
> to find an excuse to say, "Well, she's Catholic, let them take care
> of her," instead of seeing this as a larger family issue. I was there
> with them, walked with them through this, even though I am not
> their pastor and not really technically related to the mother. This
> has been an interesting case study in the lack of real connection
> of their faith that would prevent someone from [murder-suicide]
> and all the other elements that came to filter into that.[1]

To continue to pour the foundation for suicide prevention, a church must have clear life-affirming teachings focused on the value of each life and hope in the midst of suffering. Churches communicate life-affirming beliefs either through preaching or teaching. Let's see how.

Why Is Preaching and Teaching about Suicide a Problem?

Preaching and teaching are important to God's people. People go to church because their core Christian identity compels them to "live a life of faith together."[2] They want to understand their faith beliefs. Pastors and Bible teachers know how important it is to form their congregants' faith because they spend a lot of time preparing for sermons and Bible lessons. Protestant clergy spend approximately one-fourth (22 percent, or ten hours a week) of their workweek preaching (including preparation) and 13 percent of their workweek (four hours a week) teaching.[3] They spend that time because they see preaching and teaching as important to their goal of forming God's people into maturity in Christ. As Scott says, "We have an immensely holy task in front of us as we bring God's word to God's people."[4] These are holy tasks because they form God's people into a set of beliefs that affect their choices in life, into conformity to the image of Christ.

---

1. Author interview with Dr. Scott Gibson, March 25, 2021. Rev. Dr. Scott M. Gibson (DPhil, University of Oxford) holds the David E. Garland Chair of Preaching and is the director of the PhD in preaching program at Baylor University Truett Seminary. He is co-founder of the Evangelical Homiletics Society and the author or co-author of many books on preaching. He is an ordained Baptist minister.

2. Mason et al., "Unique Experiences in Religious Groups."

3. Gibson and Mason, *Preaching Hope in Darkness*, 3.

4. Gibson and Mason, *Preaching Hope in Darkness*, 125.

One of the beliefs is that God values each life. God tells us to choose life: "This day I call the heavens and the earth as witnesses against you that I have set before you life and death, blessings and curses. *Now choose life*" (Deut 30:19). But how do suicidal Christians apply this verse to their experience? Suicidal Christians may hear messages about the value of their lives, even in the midst of suffering, but not know how these messages apply to them. A military chaplain said that when he preaches, he preaches with suicidal congregants in mind. How do you do that? A pastor in another study said, "[I] think about what I'm preaching and are there moments where I can integrate 'If you're struggling with depression right now . . .'"[5] Rev. Dr. Dennis Goff of the Lutheran Foundation, Fort Wayne, Indiana, says that "accurate teaching" is crucial to suicide prevention because "it is important to know what God's word says and the value that God places on life."[6]

Suicide Isn't Mentioned

While life-affirming messages feature in preachers' sermons and teachings, how those messages apply to suicidal Christians is mostly left to these Christians to figure out. Preachers and teachers aren't helping Christians figure out how these life-affirming messages apply to them. LifeWay research found that "13 percent say their church has taught what the church believes about suicide; 14 percent say the church trained leaders to identify suicide risk factors; and 13 percent say their church shared reminders about national resources for suicide prevention."[7] Scott is sympathetic with preachers and teachers who avoid the topic of suicide. He writes,

> [Suicide is] an uncomfortable, messy and awkward topic. Perspectives on suicide may vary, even in one's congregation. We may think that to raise the topic of suicide may risk encouraging someone to go through with it. Additionally, we have limited biblical information on suicide. We're not sure about the ethical elements to suicide and its ramifications. We don't want to offend anyone, either. So, we don't talk about it. We don't preach about it. We remain silent.[8]

---

5. Unpublished interview from Mason et al., "How Counselors Can Help."
6. Unpublished interview from Mason et al., "How Counselors Can Help."
7. Smietana, "1 in 3 Protestant Churchgoers Personally Affected by Suicide."
8. Gibson and Mason, *Preaching Hope in Darkness*, 62.

A pastor in one of our studies explained that pastors are worried that mentioning suicide in church will plant the idea in a congregant's mind. He challenged a colleague, "[When you preach on adultery], do you see a spike in people having affairs?"[9] My research confirms that addressing suicide in preaching and teaching is rare. In a survey of 258 evangelical clergy and their use of suicide-prevention competencies, preaching or teaching about suicide was one of the competencies they used the least.[10] Regardless of why this happens, the message to suicidal Christians may be unintended. Jim Clemons has written, "When preachers don't address significant issues in some way, regardless of how controversial or difficult they may be, one of two messages comes thundering through the silence: either preachers don't care or they don't know what to say."[11] We saw this in chapter 2, and it bears repeating: "There are suicidal people in congregations who are listening carefully to sermons, trying to understand how faith informs their choices."[12] Suicidal congregants need to hear from pastors and Bible teachers that the Bible has something to say about suicide, and that their church cares about them enough to preach and teach on their struggles.

Preachers and teachers do not want to leave the struggles of suicidal Christians unaddressed. Jackson Carroll writes,

> The pastor's calling is to use her or his gifts and training to help members discover how biblical teachings and the church's traditions and practices apply to their lives and help them to face the challenges of the social and cultural context in which they live.[13]

It's not that the Bible has nothing to say about suicidal struggles. It's that the lack of preaching and teaching on it leaves suicidal Christians to wonder if their faith and their church are disconnected from their lived experience.[14] They may wonder if the Bible has anything to say to their struggles. Pastor Talitha insists that the Bible has plenty to say to suicidal Christians. She says,

> [The Christian] tradition has all these incredible stories of a God who is in the thick of helping with mental health issues. If the

9. Unpublished interview from Mason et al., "How Counselors Can Help."

10. Gibson and Mason, *Preaching Hope in Darkness*, 1.

11. Clemons, *Sermons on Suicide*, 8.

12. Gibson and Mason, *Preaching Hope in Darkness*, 3.

13. Carroll, *God's Potters*, 26.

14. Gibson and Mason, *Preaching Hope in Darkness*, 121.

Gospel writers saw Jesus healing people for mental health issues as so central, then the Church has got to do so as well. If people begin to hear that, then maybe the isolation from God can be bridged and healed.[15]

Addressing the Cultural Conversation

Preachers and teachers want to not only help suicidal Christians apply their faith to their experience of suicide, but they also want to engage culture to give their congregation a framework for understanding culture from their faith perspective. A pastor in one of our studies said, "Jesus criticized leaders because they couldn't understand the times they lived in."[16] Preachers and teachers have long recognized that engaging the cultural conversation is part of what happens in preaching and teaching. Scott writes,

> [Preaching] articulates God's truth and how it intersects with the culture. Preaching is vitally important to your congregants because they may not know the Bible and may be so immersed in culture that they aren't aware of how culture influences them.[17]

One of the reasons this is so important is that if preachers and teachers don't engage culture, Christians will get their information about suicide elsewhere. Pastor Tim Chang says,

> If the church cannot speak intelligibly to [cultural] issues and how Scripture informs our understanding of such issues, then we're making the gospel irrelevant. Instead, people will look to things like NPR or Fox News or Facebook or their coworker as their primary source of discipleship.[18]

Preachers and Bible teachers must engage suicide because it is part of the cultural conversation. Scott and I write, "Suicide and the language of suicide are prevalent in culture, and as pastors we want to sharpen our awareness and become increasingly free to address the matter and more comfortable

---

15. Author interview with Pastor Talitha Arnold, March 24, 2021.
16. Unpublished interview from Mason et al., "How Counselors Can Help."
17. Gibson and Mason, *Preaching Hope in Darkness*, 34.
18. Tim Chang, quoted in Gibson and Mason, *Preaching Hope in Darkness*, 22.

ministering into it."[19] As we saw in chapter 2, stigma about suicide may squelch that conversation.

What Do We Know about Preaching about Suicide in the US?

Why is it that, in general, religious people are healthier and live longer than non-religious people?[20] One reason may be that life-affirming messages get preached whether pastors and teachers intend that or not. Why? Because these messages are in the Bible. Life-affirming messages appear organically in preachers' sermons and teachings. In Philippians, Paul says that he is torn between the desire to "depart and be with Christ" and the desire to "remain in the body" (Phil 1:23), but he chooses to stay alive (v. 24). While in Philippi, he stops the jailer from killing himself: "Don't harm yourself!" (Acts 16:28). Scott adds,

> The gospel is a gospel of hope—and that is what we preach. Paul's benediction to the Roman Christians inspires to preach to those who may not think they have hope but need to hear it: "May the God of hope fill you with all joy and peace as you trust in him, so that you may overflow with hope by the power of the Holy Spirit (Rom 15:13).[21]

Preachers and Bible teachers will convey these life-affirming messages because they are in the Bible. As we saw in chapter 1, the four basic universal dimensions of religion happen organically in most churches:[22] believing,[23] bonding through rituals,[24] behaving morally,[25] and belonging.[26] Churches

19. Gibson and Mason, *Preaching Hope in Darkness*, 26.

20. VanderWeele, "Activities for Flourishing."

21. Gibson and Mason, *Preaching Hope in Darkness*, 68.

22. Saroglou, "Believing, Bonding, Behaving, and Belonging."

23. Believing (cognitive) is holding a set of beliefs about transcendent entities; i.e., something larger and more important than me exists, which is meaning-making by aiming to find the truth.

24. Bonding (emotional) is having self-transcendent, emotional experiences like awe through ritual that binds one to others and to a deeper reality that transcends the everyday reality and the self.

25. Behaving (moral) is subscribing to certain moral norms as defined *from a religious perspective*, and exerting self-control to behave in accordance with these norms and to achieve irreproachable virtue.

26. Belonging (social identity) is identifying and affiliating with a certain community or tradition, resulting in a social identity.

organically provide life-affirming beliefs that encourage choosing life, they provide communal rituals that bond people to each other and to life-affirming beliefs, and they provide a safe community to which to belong and in which to find support.

But why not preach about suicide more explicitly? Congregants touched by suicide may have to work to apply these messages to their situations. Or they may believe that suicide is irrelevant to the church or that the church is irrelevant to them. Pastors and Bible teachers can teach about suicide because it is part of some congregants' experience. It is one of their struggles. As Haddon Robinson has written, "Life-changing preaching does not talk to people about the Bible. Instead, it talks to people about themselves—their questions, hurts, fears, and struggles—from the Bible."[27] Preaching and teaching about suicide can provide a framework by which to understand suicide. One pastor told us that she preaches on suicide in order "to normalize it, to signal to the congregation that this is a safe place to talk about these types of things."[28] Scott reminds us, "Listeners are hungry for applying what you say to their lives and with each other, even in the dark places."[29]

Another reason for including suicide in preaching and teaching is that part of preaching and teaching is pastoral care. Ian MacLaren, a Scottish preacher, said to a gathering of pastors about the people to whom they preach, "Remember, everyone is having a difficult time."[30] Arthur L. Teikmanis reminds preachers, "Dynamic preaching is basically pastoral care in the context of worship."[31] Lee Eclov reflects, "Some of the best pastoral advice I ever heard, outside of Scripture, is, 'Be kind, for every person you meet is fighting a great battle.'"[32] But how do preachers and teachers preach about suicide more explicitly?

How Do We Preach about Suicide in a Church?

For a more in-depth discussion about preaching and teaching about suicide, consult our book, *Preaching Hope in Darkness: Help for Pastors in Addressing*

27. Robinson, "Blending Bible Content and Life Application," 94.

28. Unpublished interview from Mason et al., "Developmental Model."

29. Gibson and Mason, *Preaching Hope in Darkness*, 63.

30. Ian MacLaren, quoted in Gibson and Mason, *Preaching Hope in Darkness*, 63.

31. Teikmanis, *Preaching and Pastoral Care*, 19.

32. Eclov, *Pastoral Graces*, 42.

Suicide from the Pulpit. But following are some general thoughts. Overall, (former) Pastor Fe Anam Avis (whom we will meet in ch. 8) recommends "the gift of hope and love."[33]

Life-Affirming Messages

Hope in the Midst of Suffering

Scott emphasizes the good news of the gospel which gives people hope. He says, "Preaching the hope of the gospel is key to protecting against suicide."[34] He explains in my interview with him,

> Our lives are transformed. Even though we may be buffeted by all kinds of things in our own lives, from our perspective we may think it's hopeless, we still have that life-affirming gospel that says, "For God so loved the world that he gave his one and only son that whosoever believes in him might not perish but might have everlasting life." We are not those who don't have hope. We are people of hope. That's an encouragement. It's also an encouragement to know that God loves us, yes, but we are loved by others. That is part of the church. There is a concern that is expressed by the church.

Scott encourages pastors and Bible teachers to weave the hope of the gospel into the life of the church, and he explains how.

> Whether it is through Sunday School or through small groups, [weaving in the hope of the gospel] could be done. Even in the service itself, the prayers reflect this commitment, in the songs, people are reminded of it and articulate it, whether it's in the songs or the prayers themselves, or the liturgies, and in the preaching. That there is this sense, that even if you deal with difficult issues, you still have the hope of the gospel. It's always there. There are a number of layers in which this could be woven into the life of the church.

As a pastor has said, "We invite the church to understand that they are the greatest delivery system of hope in their city. . . . The church is the place that God created to manifest and distribute that hope."[35] Pastor Jack

33. Avis, *Second Day*, 112.

34. Gibson and Mason, *Preaching Hope in Darkness*, 1.

35. Mason et al., "How Counselors Can Help."

Eswine agrees this hope must be rooted in the reality of suffering. "In time, even hope demolished can become hope rebuilt, if it is realistic and rooted, not just in the cross and empty tomb but also in the garden and the sweat-like blood."[36]

What do we say about suffering? Suffering is everywhere in the Bible. Famine forced Naomi to leave the safety of her home town and then she lost her husband and two sons. She says to her neighbors when she returns,

> Don't call me Naomi, . . . Call me Mara, because the Almighty has made my life very bitter. I went away full, but the Lord has brought me back empty. Why call me Naomi? The Lord has afflicted me; the Almighty has brought misfortune upon me. (Ruth 1:20–21)

As psychologist Gay Hubbard writes, "Pain is not simply a fly that can be spooned out of life's soup."[37] In her excellent book on pain and suffering, Gay gives us perspective on Christians' pain.

> It is what it is: pain. But that is all that it is: my pain. It is not evidence of my inadequacy, my unloveableness, or the absence of my worth. It is neither proof of my personal culpability nor evidence of the absence of God . . . In this pain, I choose life. In the present darkness of my soul and disordered circumstances, I choose life. In wordless faith in an Eastering God, I choose life.[38]

Her perspective is important because suffering brings up all kinds of questions. And preachers and teachers can fuel those questions with their "should" and "ought" statements. For example, some preachers and teachers suggest that suffering is evidence of the Christian's sin (contrary to Job's righteousness in Job 31), or is evidence of the Christian's weak faith (contrary to Paul's despair in 2 Cor 1:8), or that the suffering Christian shouldn't feel bad (contrary to Jesus' anguish in Luke 22:44). There are many erroneous ideas about why and how Christians suffer and how these get communicated is crucial to listening congregants. Scott advises preachers and Bible teachers to avoid guilt-driven preaching because "our words can crush our listeners in ways that we may not be aware."[39]

So how do Christians suffer? While they remain open to joy (Hab 3:17–18), they lament to God (Psalm 13) and wait on God because he

---

36. Jack Eswine, quoted in Gibson and Mason, *Preaching Hope in Darkness*, 123.

37. Hubbard, *More Than an Aspirin*, 117.

38. Hubbard, *More Than an Aspirin*, 109–10.

39. Gibson and Mason, *Preaching Hope in Darkness*, 64.

cannot disown himself or his covenant love for us (2 Tim 2:13). And Christians maintain hope in God (Job 13:15; Rom 5:3–5; 1 Cor 13:13) in the face of their despair and anguish. Scott advises preaching and teaching hope carefully. He advises, "'You should have hope in your life,' can be reworded, 'We all want hope. You want hope, don't you?' We want to use our words to preach the gospel of grace, not guilt."[40]

An Abundant Life

Jesus said, "I have come that they may have life, and that they may have it more abundantly" (John 10:10). Some Christians read this and envision wealth and prestige. But how do we understand what Jesus meant by an abundant life? And how do suicidal Christians experience abundance? Scott says, "The hope to face today and tomorrow resides in the promise of abundant life now and in eternity."[41] Jesus was pointing to the spiritual abundance of God's provision of the Good Shepherd in our lives now and for eternity. Milton Vincent says,

> Preaching the gospel to myself each day keeps before me the startling advocacy of God for my fullness, and it also serves as a means by which I feast anew on the fullness of provision that God has given to me in Christ.[42]

Suicidal Christians can face life's challenges with the understanding that God is present with them because of his enduring love and tender care for them.

Some suicidal Christians are dealing with mental illness, which may not feel like an abundant life. God is present in these challenges, too. One of our study participants said,

> We can now look at major characters in the Hebrew Bible and show that they were depressed. Does God punish them for those thoughts? No. Most often God sends people to help. And telling these stories is protective because, for one thing, people see that they are not the only ones who feel that way.[43]

---

40. Gibson and Mason, *Preaching Hope in Darkness*, 65.

41. Gibson and Mason, *Preaching Hope in Darkness*, 67.

42. Vincent, *Gospel Primer*, 45, 47.

43. Mason et al., "How Counselors Can Help."

How do suicidal Christians build lives worth living? Suicidal Christians can build lives worth living founded on the knowledge of God's love for them and God's presence with them.

In addition, the Bible tells us that dedicating our lives to God, inviting him to be our north star, affects every aspect of our lives. When we live life for God, we lean on him for guidance (Prov 3:5–6, 16:9; John 16:13: Jas 1:5). We express gratitude to him for his love and goodness (Psalm 100). We conduct our relationships and our work in the context of God's love for us (Eccl 2:24–25, 5:19, 9:9–10, 12:13). Research has found that all these activities contribute to life satisfaction, well-being, less depression, and flourishing.[44] That is what an abundant life is. That is a life worth living. Suicidal Christians and Christians with mental illness are as capable of building these types of lives as Christians who are not suicidal or do not have mental illness. Scott recommends in-depth study of the Bible to understand what the good life is.

> In small groups or in Sunday School, there [could be] a book study or a Bible study on the good life, the *good* life. What is life and what does this all look like? Say the book of Philippians. It's a small snapshot about a church, the struggles that they had, but that book is full of hope. It is an encouraging book. If you could study those kinds of things that help to show a life-affirming [message]. If you have that perspective, you can look through that lens at various writings of Scripture and see "This is what the Scriptures are affirming. It is affirming a life that is dedicated to God. There is this sense that this is what a good life looks like. It's a life of abundance, one of hope, one that respects life." . . . And I think too that a neglected area of doing that is in the younger kids. I am one who thinks that one of the things we've lost out on is the matter of catechizing, using a catechism. Some type of catechism needs to be developed. It's not long but some type of catechism that could be developed that would cover the basics of faith but also underscore the value of life and living that life to the glory of God. That's what the first statement in the Westminster catechism is: "Glorify God and enjoy him forever." That's a great start. There are different layers that that could be woven into the fabric of people's lives a lot earlier and throughout the life of the church.

44. Bolier et al., "Positive Psychology Interventions"; Seligman et al., "Positive Psychology Progress"; Sheldon and Lyubomirsky, "How to Increase and Sustain Positive Emotion."

More Life-Affirming Messages

In *Preaching Hope in Darkness,* Scott and I have laid out how to preach on hope and suffering, and five more preaching and teaching topics that can help prevent suicide.[45] Appendix H in *Preaching Hope in Darkness* lays out how to teach these topics in youth and young adult Bible studies.[46] Here are topics for preaching and teaching that keep suicidal congregants in mind:

1. *Connection to others*: "One of the most hopeless situations for suicidal Christians is that they have lost a sense of having strong bonds with others."[47] You can preach or teach on God's presence with us at all times and especially in our suffering, and that as Christians we belong to each other (Rom 12:5).

2. *Worth and dignity of every person*: A second hopeless situation for suicidal Christians is "their enduring self-hatred, their sense of being a burden, or the sense that their significant others would be better off without them."[48] This perspective needs to be balanced with the Christian perspective that being made in the image of God (Gen 1:27–28) means (humans) can't lose their worth and dignity. "Paul prevents the suicide of the Philippian jailer (Acts 16:25–40). In verse twenty-eight, Paul shouts, 'Do not harm yourself!' even though it was that jailer who had imprisoned Paul and Silas. Death is the enemy even for a jailer (1 Cor 15:25–26)."[49]

3. *Hope*: "Pastors cannot help but soak their congregants in hope because the Bible is full of 'narratives of hope.'"[50] "In the Bible, when everything looks hopeless, God repeatedly intervenes mightily and redeems the bad into something good (Prov 16:4). In Genesis 50:20, Joseph tells his brothers that though what they did was evil, God used it to produce a great good, the salvation of Israel from famine. . . . The pervasive massage of the Bible is that there is always hope."[51]

45. Gibson and Mason, *Preaching Hope in Darkness,* 41–56.

46. Gibson and Mason, *Preaching Hope in Darkness,* 199–230.

47. Gibson and Mason, *Preaching Hope in Darkness,* 41.

48. Gibson and Mason, *Preaching Hope in Darkness,* 43.

49. Gibson and Mason, *Preaching Hope in Darkness,* 49.

50. Kaplan and Schwartz, *Psychology of Hope.*

51. Gibson and Mason, *Preaching Hope in Darkness,* 46.

4. *Moral objections to suicide and reasons to live*: "Most pastors believe that suicide is morally wrong.[52] Suicidal people need their own moral objections to suicide. A moral objection to suicide is a conviction that suicide is forbidden by God";[53] "A suicidal person may already know the moral objections to suicide but not all the steps to building a life worth living."[54]

5. *Self-control and the habit of choosing life*: Some researchers believe that the reason religion protects against suicide is that it teaches self-control.[55] "Congregants use self-control to regulate or adjust their behavior to match a standard of behavior. In the case of suicide, the standard is to choose life."[56]

6. *Grief and suffering*: "It is difficult to avoid preaching and teaching on suffering because Christians have never been immune to suffering";[57] "Preaching and teaching on suffering can help suicidal people make sense out of their suffering."[58] Preaching and teaching can show suffering Christians how to manage their suffering and how to come alongside others in the midst of their suffering.

7. *Encouragement to reach out for help*: As we saw in chapter 2, pastors lead the way in developing a transparent, authentic community where congregants can reach out for help without risking judgment. "Fearing judgment results in superficial relationships where congregants feel alone with their brokenness and don't reach out when they need help."[59]

Regular Attendance

These life-affirming messages are communicated either subtly or explicitly in the preaching and teaching in a church. Why is it that those

---

52. Mason et al., "Moral Deliberations."

53. Gibson and Mason, *Preaching Hope in Darkness*, 48.

54. Gibson and Mason, *Preaching Hope in Darkness*, 49.

55. McCullough and Willoughby, "Religion, Self-Regulation, and Self-Control."

56. Gibson and Mason, *Preaching Hope in Darkness*, 50.

57. Gibson and Mason, *Preaching Hope in Darkness*, 52.

58. Gibson and Mason, *Preaching Hope in Darkness*, 53.

59. Gibson and Mason, *Preaching Hope in Darkness*, 54.

who attend church *at least weekly* are over five times less likely to die by suicide?[60] Regular attendance ensures that these messages will be heard. Scott reflected on his story:

> I'm not sure how much [the military man] cultivated his spiritual life since his initial coming into the Catholic Church when he went through CCD [Co-fraternity of Christian Doctrine] classes, which would have been around twelve years old. I think for people who are really wrestling with suicidal ideation who are part of a church, and really involved in a church, going to worship on Sunday morning at least, they are exposed to more hope, more connectedness, than somebody who isn't. That person has a lot more exposure to doctrine, a lot more exposure to developing a more firm foundation, than somebody who is not, like my aunt who had no hope. All she had was herself.

Tangible Pastoral Care

Scott adds that messages of hope come through not only explicit words in a sermon or Bible lesson, but in tangible pastoral care. The pastor is the embodiment of Jesus' love for his flock as the Good Shepherd. The pastor demonstrates in a tangible way God's tender care for his people. How do pastors and teachers do that for suicidal congregants? Scott suggests,

> We pray for someone and we let the person know we're praying. But what else could you do for that person? Well, you could send a card. You could call him or her on the phone or "let's meet for lunch" or "come over to our house for dinner." Whatever it might be. What are the tangible kinds of things that express a connection to community so that the folks don't think that they are alone? That's the thing that churches need to be pushed on.

Scott gives more examples of tangible pastoral care. He says,

> I remember when my father died. My father was an alcoholic and a difficult person. I was living out of state. I went back to my home. When I got there, standing on the porch was this old farmer. His name was Art Glasser. When I got out of my car, he just wrapped his arms around me. And I bawled my eyes out. And my home church came there and stepped in and brought food. My mom and my father had nothing to do with the church, but my church

---

60. VanderWeele, "Activities for Flourishing."

had everything to do with me. The church extended themselves in an incredible way. I'll never forget my brother-in-law said to me, "I cannot believe what this church has done for us." He couldn't believe the love and the expressions of love that this church had for me, for them. That's what a church does. They weren't sophisticated folks, but they were sophisticated in Christ. They understood how to reach out. They reached out to drug addicts and loved them. That's the kind of church I'd like to see all churches become, a church that is sensitive to the needs of people. Helping a drug addict was outside of their comfort zone. They helped an addict get ladders to become a house painter. They gave him jobs at their houses and paid him. He got on his feet. It was astounding. They saw the value of the person and the need that the person had and they met it. This church still does that. They reach out and help people in ways that are amazing.

Scott makes the point that sometimes congregants need evidence of God's love through tangible pastoral care and through the love of the church. Pastor Amy (from ch. 2) agrees, "Sometimes we need the community around us to believe that God cares."

Vulnerability: We're All Sinners

This willingness on the part of the church to reach out to suicidal congregants comes from each congregant's recognition of their own brokenness and vulnerability to sin. When I asked Scott how he understands what "deep community"[61] in a church is, this is what he said:

[A deep community is] a church that itself has understood hurt and pain and they've come to terms with it as a church. They know people aren't perfect. When [my home church's] treasurer embezzled money and the church found out, she repented and the church forgave her. They didn't give her the job of treasurer again. But she went on to become a much more mature Christian. The church came to terms with the fact that people are sinful and they are a community of forgiveness. That's what they needed to do. No church is perfect. . . . It's a church that recognizes its own vulnerability. They are all vulnerable no matter what. When you come to terms with that, you realize that nobody is perfect. That doesn't give you an excuse to not move on towards maturity, but it doesn't set you up for disappointment too badly.

61. Unpublished interview from Mason et al., "How Counselors Can Help."

Scott explains that this vulnerability feeds hope. "No matter who you are, you can become a follower of Christ and become somebody who is forgiven even when you disappoint each other and the Savior." Care is a reflection of the gospel of hope. A pastor participant in one of our studies said,

> [Suicidal people] need to know that Jesus meets them in the middle of the suicidal ideation and provides them with help and hope in the context of the church, instilling hope. If we, as a Christian community, don't point people to Jesus and the hope we have in him, not as the Band-Aid that makes everything okay, but it does allow us to live in the moment and look forward to the next moment knowing that we are not alone.[62]

But how does a church get to the place where they are willing to embrace their vulnerability to sin and their willingness to embrace all congregants, even suicidal congregants? Scott describes how pastoral care supported the preaching.

> It wasn't necessarily the preaching that got the church there, except that there was a strong pastoral tone in a number of the pastors. There was a real caring that was communicated in the *ethos* of the pastor. That really made a difference. That *ethos* trickled down from the pulpit and affected everybody else and how they dealt with each other. It almost sets a pattern. If you have a sharp-edged, hard angled approach, that is going to be reflected in the people. What was modeled was a real pastoral care and concern. That provides hope and reflects the gospel. It encourages people to maturity.

Will Willimon agrees,

> A key factor in whether the liturgy works is the pastor's leadership. The presider of the liturgy sets the tone of the assembly, educates by his very presence and attitude, provides coherence and unity to the community's celebrations, helps move the congregation toward its desired goal, and reminds the congregation under whose grace and judgment we all stand.[63]

Preaching and teaching the life-affirming messages from the Bible are foundational to a church-based approach to suicide prevention. In the next chapter, we'll finish pouring the foundation by showing how worship helps

---

62. Unpublished interview from Mason et al., "How Counselors Can Help."

63. Willimon, *Worship as Pastoral Care,* 214.

prevent suicide. Because preaching and teaching happen in the context of worship, we might reflect on how preaching and teaching life-affirming messages differ from worship. Will Willimon differentiates between the two by saying that being a congregation's preacher is "to expand [congregants'] knowledge of and practice of the faith," but being their priest in worship is "to stand with them before God, to mediate between their lives and loves and the life and love of the Almighty."[64] Preaching and teaching are different from worship. And preaching and teaching overlap with worship. Dr. Dave Currie writes that "all preaching is worship"[65] and "all worship is preaching."[66] Let's see how worship helps prevent suicide.

Discussion Questions

1. What does the culture say about suicide? How does the church engage these messages?

2. A military chaplain said he preaches with the assumption that a suicidal person is listening. How could preachers and teachers keep suicidal Christians in mind?

3. How might suicidal Christians think the church is irrelevant to them or that suicide is irrelevant to the church?

4. When Jesus says he came to give abundant life, what did he mean? How would suicidal Christians build lives worth living?

5. What other sermon and teaching topics would help suicidal Christians build lives worth living?

Take Stock of Your Church

1. What messages are suicidal Christians hearing at your church?

2. What view of suffering does your church preach and teach?

3. Has the word "suicide" ever been mentioned in your church's preaching and teaching? Where and when?

64. Willimon, *Worship as Pastoral Care*, 9–10.

65. Currie, *Big Idea of Biblical Worship*, loc. 152.

66. Currie, *Big Idea of Biblical Worship*, loc. 172.

4. Where in the preaching and teaching might it make sense to speak the word "suicide"?

5. How might suicidal people in your church react to hearing the word "suicide" said out loud in church? How might they react if the word "suicide" is never spoken?

6. How does your church display tangible care for suicidal Christians?

7. How does your church display vulnerability to sin and brokenness?

8. How does your church display pastoral care to suicidal Christians?

Resources

Gibson, Scott, and Karen Mason. *Preaching Hope in Darkness: Help for Pastors in Addressing Suicide from the Pulpit*. Bellingham: Lexham, 2020.
988 Suicide & Crisis Lifeline. https://988lifeline.org/

CHAPTER 4

Essential Element 3: A Worshipping Church

> Sing praises to God, sing praises; sing praises to our King, sing
> praises. (Ps 47:6)

Pastor Talitha Arnold says, "My family was affected by suicide and suicide attempt." Her father was discharged from the military in World War II
with undiagnosed post-traumatic stress disorder ("battle fatigue," as it was
called then). Both her parents were environmental scientists, but when her
father's research on bald eagle conservation was squelched in the 1950s, his
mental health condition worsened. He was hospitalized for several years.
When he was allowed out on a pass, he died. The coroner ruled his death
a suicide. But the family didn't talk about suicide. Pastor Talitha was much
older before she even heard the "unspoken family story" that he had died
by suicide. Later, when she was in seventh grade, another family member
began to manifest a mental health condition and attempted suicide.

> The next day, we all went back to school. You didn't talk about it.
> And I sure didn't talk about it at church. Seventh grade was also
> when I dropped out of church. It wasn't because of teenage rebel-
> lion, but it was because I didn't feel like I belonged in church. I
> thought the mental health issues were my fault because I couldn't
> always "turn the other cheek" or "go the extra mile." I thought if I'd
> been more loving, more understanding, more "Christian," every-
> thing would have been okay.

She has also seen that faith communities can blame the person and the
families for mental illness. Some might say, "It's a sin and if you just prayed
enough, it would change." Or churches don't talk about it at all. "The shame,
the stigma that fell on my mother because of my father's death also fell on
the family. I never talked about it at church. I never talked about it with
anybody except one family friend and my 4H leader. None of my teachers

knew." She says, "When the church could not talk about mental illness or suicide, then it felt like God couldn't either."

During Talitha's first year in seminary, the spouse of a professor died by suicide. Talitha sang with the chapel choir at the funeral, where suicide was never mentioned, though everyone knew the spouse had died by suicide. She says,

> That was a very clear signal that this was not something you are supposed to talk about. Just as with the church, when the seminary couldn't even say the words "suicide" or "mental illness," it felt like God couldn't deal with such things either.

Pastor Talitha didn't talk about mental health publicly until she took an associate pastor position. This breakthrough happened when the senior minister asked her to preach a Lenten series on the healing stories of Jesus. Jesus' first healing in Mark (Mark 1:21–28) was the cleansing of the man with the unclean spirit. In her Bible study, she realized that the number of times Jesus healed people with a first-century description of a mental health condition far outnumbered all the other healings combined. "That was a real epiphany." She decided that she couldn't preach that sermon without being honest about her story. (In chapter 2, Pastor Talitha provides guidance about telling publicly a personal story of suicide.) Jesus separated the illness from the man when Jesus speaks to the unclean spirit, not to the man. She remembers, "Jesus responds with compassion, with care, with the goal to restore the person to their right mind and to their community." That realization was powerful for her. In the next week or two, people came out of the woodwork to share their story or their family's story with her. "Finally somebody had opened up the conversation and it was okay." It was the first time in her life that she had heard a sermon that used the words mental illness and suicide "and it was a sermon I preached." The church followed the sermon with some adult forums and education on mental illness which "began to open things up." Seeing the body of Christ try to come together every Sunday "warts and all" is what got Pastor Talitha excited about parish ministry. She has seen that congregations have become more honest about mental health conditions because "life has forced them to become more honest."

The experience of not feeling there was a place for her and her family in church has fueled her commitment to try to make the church inclusive. Growing up in a single mother family, she knows what it feels like to be an outsider. "There is some inkling that you have to pay attention to that and that extends to people dealing with mental health issues or in their family." She has let her current church know that this is a place where people can talk about mental illness and suicide.

Pastor Talitha Arnold is a founding member of the Executive Committee of the National Action Alliance for Suicide Prevention. She founded and co-led the Faith Communities Task Force for many years. She has been the pastor of United Church of Christ in Santa Fe, New Mexico, since 1987. United Church is known in Santa Fe for its vital worship and diverse music. She believes in the power of worship with is "engaging, lively, honest, at the very heart of our life together, as a major suicide prevention work" of the church. Pastor Talitha will help us engage this question of how worship helps prevent suicide.

In this chapter, we'll finish pouring the foundation for the prevention of suicide in a church. We'll talk about the importance of worship, which includes worship singing, praise, prayer, reading sacred Scriptures, giving an offering, and rhythms in the life of the church. While both personal and communal worship are important, we'll focus on why worship as a community is vital to protecting against suicide.

Why Is Worship a Problem?

The problem with some worship is that it can bind congregants together into some inaccurate beliefs. Some Christians believe (like Job's friends) that suffering only happens because the suffering person sinned. That's just not consistent with the Bible. Christians have never been immune to suffering (2 Cor 1:8; 1 Pet 4:12). Jesus was himself "a man of suffering and familiar with pain" (Isa 53:3). A lot of people of faith lived difficult lives and died horrible deaths (Heb 11:36–38) without being rescued by God (Heb 11:39). We are groaning and waiting eagerly for the redemption of our bodies (Rom 8:23), and for heaven (Rev 21:4). Pastor Talitha says, "The message to my family was that if we were just more loving, more caring, better Christians, everything, or our family, would be okay." This belief is not only inconsistent with the Bible, but also damaging to people touched by suicide.

Worship can communicate that all you have to do is bring your suffering to God and he'll solve it, which contradicts the empirically verifiable fact of original sin and suffering.[1] If God is expected to solve Christians' problems, then people who suffer conclude something is wrong with

---

1. Finstuen, *Original Sin and Everyday Protestants.*

them. This is unfair to suffering congregants and is not consistent with the Bible. As the Spencers help us understand, in James 5:14–15, we are promised forgiveness of sins which "has no doubt of fulfillment,"[2] but healing does have some doubt of fulfillment.

Some Christians teach that suffering is good. Suffering is not good in itself. In Lamentations 3:33, we read that God does not willingly allow suffering. Pastor Talitha says, "The other part of the family story was that my father's death or the other mental health issues were God's way of making us stronger, which makes God into a sadist." Suffering won't exist in God's new heaven and new earth (Rev 21:4).

Some Christians believe that Christians don't feel pain. But suffering is painful. The Bible captures a breadth of emotions experienced by suffering people: anger (Ps 7:11; Mark 3:5; John 2:15–16; Eph 4:26), anguish and bitterness (1 Sam 1:10), anxiety (Ps 6:7; 2 Cor 7:7; Phil 2:26–28), despondency (Ps 42:5, 11; Ps 43:5; Ps 88), distress (1 Sam 22:2; 2 Sam 22:7; 2 Kgs 4:27), fear (Matt 14:26–30), grief (2 Sam 19:4), guilt (Matt 27:3), indignation (Ps 137), longing (Ps 38:9; Prov 13:12), and sorrow (Ps 6:7; Jer 20:18), to name a few. The Psalmist says, "I am in distress, my eyes grow weak with sorrow, my soul and body with grief. My life is consumed by anguish and my years by groaning; my strength fails because of my affliction" (Ps 31:9–10).

Worship can communicate to suffering people that if their faith were stronger or if they prayed more, they wouldn't be struggling. As we saw in chapter 2 (but it bears repeating), psychologist Gay Hubbard challenges that perspective:

> Contrary to [the thinking that "He'll fix it so I won't have to live through it,"] God refuses to play the magician's role, nor is God in the business of providing free placebos or heavenly strength aspirin. The idea that if we can only get our burdens to God He will make us instantly feel better is bitterly unfair misdirection to people in pain . . . this "fix-it" approach makes pain a measure of our distance from God. Indirectly, this idea encourages us to think, "If I hurt, I'm a long way from God. If I were close to Him, He would make the hurt go away." The God of all comfort . . . is an identity quite different . . . from the idea of God as the "Great Pain Reliever."[3]

2. Spencer and Spencer, *Joy through the Night*, 127.

3. Hubbard, *More Than an Aspirin*, 91.

Worship is one of the ways some of these inaccurate beliefs get communicated, and worship is a way to challenge them. Jesus tells us to worship "in spirit and in truth" (John 4:23). Truth is part of worship. One of the truths is that humans suffer and suffering is painful. Pastor Talitha says,

> Music connects us with people who have also gone through hard, hard times. One of the reasons I returned to the Christian church is that I found an honesty in the African American spirituals and gospel songs that I wasn't finding in my own white tradition about the human condition.

But she also found a different approach to suffering. She adds,

> It was through the civil rights movement, of seeing that a God who caused or sanctioned suffering was not the God of Rosa Parks, Martin Luther King Jr., or others. They looked to the story of the Exodus and to the God who hears the cries of the Hebrews and brings them out of slavery into freedom. Parks, King, and the African American community weren't doing anything "wrong." Nor were they innately "sinful." They do not deserve the punishment, the suffering that has been inflicted upon them or upon their ancestors. God did not will that. Instead, God was standing with them and empowering them to march to freedom, to end the suffering. Once I started to think about that, over a couple of decades, I began to realize that God is not a God who causes suffering—including the suffering of mental illness. Suffering happens because we are finite human beings with finite minds and finite bodies and finite levels of compassion. I think worship can remind us of that in a profound kind of way.

Pastor Talitha emphasizes that truthfulness in worship reduces our isolation from God and church.

What Do We Know about Worship?

Dr. Dave Currie writes that

> [Biblical worship] is raised up when the *whole* word of God guides the *whole* person, together with the *whole* people of God, into the *full* presence of the Father, in *full* union with the Son, through the *full* power of the Holy Spirit to further the *fulfilment* of the *whole* mission of God.[4]

---

4. Currie, *Big Idea of Biblical Worship*, loc. 303.

He writes that the goal of worship is "to be drawn into the Father's presence as fully as finite, fallen and redeemed creatures can be."[5] He adds, "We don't worship God as a means to any other end, but simply to delight in the One who is worthy of worship."[6]

Worship is everything we do in our lives that glorifies God. "So whether you eat or drink or whatever you do, do it all for the glory of God" (1 Cor 10:31). Worship can be what we offer to God individually. But it is also what we do in church collectively (Heb 10:25). Worship in church is what we do when we congregate together as a body of Christ. While worship can include many components like a prayer of invocation, a call to confession, and benediction,[7] we will focus on the components of praising God through music (1 Chr 20:19; Eph 5:18–20; Col 3:16), speaking praises (Ps 34:1; Ps 103:1-2; Heb 13:15), Bible reading (1 Tim 4:13), prayer (2 Chr 6:40; Rev 8:4), words of instruction like a sermon (1 Cor 14:26), giving an offering (Deut 16:16–17; Prov 3:9), and rhythms in the life of the church like the Lord's Supper (Acts 2:42).

Congregated worship does a lot of good. Pastor Talitha says, "There is something about singing with other people. . . . [Through singing] we are trying to get faith inside people. Sometimes you can do it better with a song, than you can with a lesson."[8] Researchers have found that people who walked, sang, or moved their arms in synchrony with each other showed greater liking, trust, cooperation, and self-sacrifice than groups performing the same behaviors while not in synchrony.[9] In worship, congregants sing, speak, listen, pray, give an offering, and enact rhythms in the life of the church in synchrony. Activities with synchronous body movements help group members feel more oneness with their group.[10] The synchrony of worship binds religious people into a religious community.[11] Émile Durkheim, a sociologist, believed that religion prevents suicide because of the common practices that create the collective life of the church.[12] These

5. Currie, *Big Idea of Biblical Worship*, Kindle 14 percent.

6. Currie, *Big Idea of Biblical Worship*, Kindle 15 percent.

7. Currie, *Big Idea of Biblical Worship*, Kindle 17 percent.

8. Unpublished interview from Mason et al., "How Counselors Can Help."

9. Wiltermuth and Heath, "Synchrony and Cooperation."

10. Fischer et al., "How Do Rituals Affect Cooperation?"

11. Graham and Haidt, "Beyond Beliefs."

12. Durkheim, *Suicide*, 125.

communal rhythms help keep Christians committed to their faith[13] and bind congregants to each other,[14] deepening group cohesion.[15] Pastor Talitha explains that worship connects congregants to

> an intentional community that bears the responsibility for caring, for compassion, for accepting people where they are in their journey. It provides a community that if I don't show up, somebody might actually reach out and say, "We missed you today."

Pastor Amy (from ch. 2) cautions that suicidal congregants who feel disconnected from their church might have the opposite experience,

> In faith communities, you run the risk [of] having a place where I am supposed to feel connected, but I feel alone because nobody talks to me or my relationships are all superficial, so that I end up feeling more alone. But now it is alone in a crowd, and alone in a crowd is the worst kind.[16]

Rev. Dr. Dennis Goff of the Lutheran Foundation, Fort Wayne, Indiana, adds, "I want to feel [God's value of my life] from my faith community, and I want to feel like the people around me value me."[17] If that is not part of the experience of the suicidal congregant, worship may not protect from suicide.

Worship binds congregants to their pastors, who stay in tune with their congregation during worship. Pastor Talitha clarifies,

> The amount of pastoral information I pick up on a Sunday morning within a five-hour period, a few services, and children's ministry and education, is enormous. The amount of pastoral contact I can have on a Sunday is enormous. I can see somebody is sitting in a new place. Somebody is crying at the end of the sermon (and it wasn't that bad of a sermon). You scan the congregation and you pick up a lot of important pastoral information. People come through the line or they don't come through the line and they always come through the line. You just pick up those kind of pastoral clues.

---

13. Atran and Henrich, "Evolution of Religion."

14. Paladino et al., "Synchronous Multisensory Stimulation"; Tajadura-Jiménez et al., "Other in Me."

15. Xygalatas et al., "Extreme Rituals Promote Prosociality."

16. Unpublished interview from Mason et al., "How Counselors Can Help."

17. Unpublished interview from Mason et al., "How Counselors Can Help."

Will Willimon agrees, "Priests and pastors have the vantage point from whence to get a firsthand, official view of the lack of community, the difficulties of community, and the separateness within the community they serve."[18] This kind of congregational care happens only in church. Christians must worship communally, not just individually.

Worship not only helps prevent suicide because of the mutual care, but also because it binds congregants to their faith tradition. A researcher found that worship activities that were full of emotional energy, satisfaction, and group belonging were associated with congregants being more likely to retain commitment to the religious group, resulting in stronger religious tradition affiliation.[19] A study participant points to the "sense of shared purpose, shared values" as helping to prevent suicide.[20] One of the "shared values" that suicidal congregants may need to hear constantly in worship is that, as Pastor Talitha says, "God is a living God who is involved in their lives and cares about them and loves them."[21] As Will Willimon writes, "Worship has no other function than the joyful, ecstatic abandon that comes when we meet and are met by God."[22] He adds,

> By rhythmically engaging ourselves in familiar ritual, we are freed to moments of true spontaneity and ecstasy. Part of the value of well-defined and familiar ritual is that we do not have to think about it. We lose ourselves within the familiar words and gestures so that our minds are free to roam and play in unknown territory of the psyche. Our mind wanders to the important things we usually do not have time or courage to think about.[23]

In the experience of worship, a suicidal Christian may be bound to a deeper reality that transcends the everyday reality and the self.[24] Worship binds congregants to their faith.

You might wonder, does prayer have to be communal or could it be individual? A researcher[25] studied the effect of collective prayer. He found that communal prayer was distinct from, and not simply an aggregate of,

18. Willimon, *Worship as Pastoral Care*, 206.

19. Baker, "Social Sources of the Spirit."

20. Unpublished interview from Mason et al., "How Counselors Can Help."

21. Unpublished interview from Mason et al., "How Counselors Can Help."

22. Willimon, *Worship as Pastoral Care*, 47.

23. Willimon, *Worship as Pastoral Care*, 177.

24. Saroglou, "Believing, Bonding, Behaving, and Belonging."

25. Fuist, "Talking to God."

individual prayer. This is consistent with one of our study participants who said,

> Prayer gives people strength. . . . I think that if you are actually regularly involving yourself with some kind of practice and communal prayer, . . . you're forced, if you are being mindful of what you are doing . . . to consider yourself in relation to all sorts of things that are much bigger than you.[26]

How Do We Prevent Suicide in a Church through Worship?

As we've seen, all worship can help prevent suicide through binding congregants together,[27] to their pastor, and binding them to their faith. Any worship done with other congregants can help prevent suicide. Pastor Scott (from ch. 3) writes,

> The act of worship—giving thanks in word, expressing praise in song, praying to the Lord, listening to the preached Word—encourages the deepening of faith, bolstering believers to face the challenges of life with renewed strength. Worship engenders an appreciation of life and hope. Thoughtful, prayerful worship planning is key to inspiring hope in the prevention of suicide.[28]

But what are some examples of worship that explicitly addresses suicide? As Pastor Amy (from ch. 2) says, "There are some things that should be named clearly."[29]

Praising God through Music

Kurt Carr's song "I Almost Let Go" is a powerful worship song that binds congregants to the life-affirming message that God holds people close and doesn't let them go in their most difficult moments.

> I felt like I couldn't take life anymore
>
> My problems had me bound
>
> Depression weighed me down

---

26. Mason et al., "How Counselors Can Help."

27. Holt-Lunstad et al., "Loneliness and Social Isolation as Risk Factors."

28. Gibson and Mason, *Preaching Hope in Darkness*, 70–71.

29. Unpublished interview from Mason et al., "How Counselors Can Help."

> But God held me close
> So I wouldn't let go
> God's mercy kept me
> So I wouldn't let go.[30]

A congregant contemplating suicide may find this song's life-affirming message relevant to their struggles.

Speaking Praises

We speak our praises to God by giving him thanks for his blessings (1 Chr 16:34; Ps 35:18; 1 Thess 5:18). Worship gives congregants opportunity to speak praises which promote well-being and counteract depression and mortality.[31] In these praises, people count blessings[32] and express gratitude.[33] Jackson elaborates,

> The act of giving thanks helps to bring life back into balance by weighing the blessings against misfortunes. Though no life is free of its disturbances, there are multitudes of things and people and happenings for which one can truly be thankful. We need the reality to see life as it is and not as it may seem to be. That person who finds not opportunity for thankfulness is neither fair to himself nor to life in general when he begins to count his misfortunes. That person who has learned the art of thankfulness learns life's quiet satisfactions, and finds a balance that tends to discount anything that would destroy right relations with his Creator.[34]

This song by Johnson Oatman Jr. (1897) captures gratitude for God's blessings.

> When upon life's billows you are tempest-tossed,
> When you are discouraged, thinking all is lost,
> Count your many blessings, name them one by one,
> And it will surprise you what the Lord has done.

30. Kurt Carr, "I Almost Let Go," track 2 on *WOW Gospel*, Kcartunes, 2004. Used with permission.

31. Bolier et al., "Positive Psychology Interventions."

32. Emmons and McCullough, "Counting Blessings versus Burdens"; Seligman et al., "Positive Psychology Progress."

33. Seligman et al., "Positive Psychology Progress"; Sheldon and Lyubomirsky, "How to Increase and Sustain Positive Emotion."

34. Jackson, *Psychology for Preaching*, 86.

> Count your blessings, name them one by one,
> Count your blessings, see what God has done!

Children who attend worship one hour per week do better in many areas of life, including grades and reduced risk of suicide.[35] Worship might help prevent suicide by helping people flourish through generating positive emotions, engagement, relationships, and meaning.[36] Worship activities are similar to those that increase life satisfaction[37] through increasing meaning and purpose,[38] which reduces mortality.[39] As one study participant faith leader said, "the faith community offers a sense of wholeness, if you want to think about it that way, that there is meaning to my life and God has a purpose for me."[40] However, these praises need to be balanced by the reality that some psalms (see Psalm 88) do not include praise. Sometimes suffering Christians will not be in a place to offer up gratitude.

Giving an Offering

In Deuteronomy 8:10–18, God reminds us that everything we have is his gift to us. God warns the people of Israel and us: "You may say to yourself, 'My power and the strength of my hands have produced this wealth for me.' But remember the Lord your God, for it is he who gives you the ability to produce wealth, and so confirms his covenant, which he swore to your ancestors, as it is today." When we give an offering, we remind ourselves of God's good gifts to us, a blessing we can count.

Bible Reading

Pastor Talitha has said that pastors cannot help but soak their congregants in hope because the Bible is full of narratives of hope like Hagar (Gen 16:6–16, 21:8–20), Joseph (Gen 50:20), Moses (Num 11:10–15), Hannah (First Samuel 1); Elijah (First Kings 19), and Tamar, Rahab, and Ruth

---

35. See the website for Take Me to Worship: https://www.takemetoworship.org//stats-facts.

36. Seligman, *Flourish*.

37. VanderWeele et al., "Reimagining Health."

38. Cohen et al., "Purpose in Life."

39. Martín-María et al., "Impact of Subjective Well-Being."

40. Unpublished interview from Mason et al., "How Counselors Can Help."

(Matt 1:1–17).[41] In these narratives, God tangibly shows his compassion to suffering people by supplying practical helps like food and water to Hagar and seventy elders to Moses, and thereby renews their hope. Reading these narratives of hope and pointing out God's compassion to suffering people can help give hope to suicidal congregants. Reading about hope helps congregants understand that hope is as important a Christian virtue as faith and love (1 Cor 13:13).

Prayer

One way to include suicide explicitly in prayer is to join the National Action Alliance campaign for the National Weekend of Prayer for Faith, Hope, and Life.[42] On one weekend a year, churches across the US join together to pray for people touched by suicide. Observe the National Action Alliance Weekend of Prayer or Mental Health Awareness Month or World Suicide Prevention Day. Pastor Amy (from ch. 2) said, "I think suicide should be included at least once a year."

However, many churches are beginning to pray explicitly for those who struggle with a mental health condition. A study participant said,

> We use open prayer, before church, for anybody who needs someone in the community to pray for them and one of the things we pray for in that time is anybody who is struggling with depression or anxiety and that's just a normal thing to be praying for.[43]

Pastor Talitha adds, "In prayers I always make sure that when we're praying for 'those who are afflicted in mind, soul or body, walking through the valleys of the shadows.'"

And some are praying explicitly for those who have thoughts of suicide. A study participant recommended, "Include in prayer, those who are struggling with thoughts of suicide, or people who have made an attempt and are now battling for life, the same way we would for someone who has an illness." Another gave the example, "It is not uncommon for us to have somebody during prayers say, 'Please pray for me. I'm having thoughts of suicide.'"

---

41. Mason et al., "Developmental Model"; Gibson and Mason, *Preaching Hope in Darkness*, 46.

42. See their website: https://theactionalliance.org.

43. Unpublished interview from Mason et al., "How Counselors Can Help."

Prayers are powerful signals that God cares for people struggling with suicide. Scott and I give these examples of corporate responsive prayers in *Preaching Hope in Darkness.*

> We pray to you, Father, for all those in despair
> *That they would choose life*
> For those facing devastating loss
> *That they would remember your presence and intercession for them*
> For all those who feel they are a burden
> *That they would love themselves as you love them*
> For all those without hope
> *That they would find in you, Father, a reason to live*
> For those who feel alone
> *That they would find in our gathered community a reason to live*
> For those facing evil in this world
> *That they would remember your redemption of the evil done*
> *to Joseph.*
> For all those suffering the misery of depression and other
> psychological pain
> *That they would reach out for help like Blind Bartimaeus*
> For all those in despondent desolation
> *That we would reach out to them*[44]

> Almighty God, you alone give life and take it but life is not easy. With the psalmist, we proclaim that without you, we would be swallowed alive, torn up and engulfed by the floods and swept away by the torrents of this life. Preserve us, Father. We put our hope in you, Father, Son and Holy Spirit. Amen.[45]

Words of Instruction Like a Sermon

As Scott and I write,[46] preaching and teaching about suicide can be challenging.

> There are reasons why we don't preach on suicide. We may be reluctant to bring it up. It's an uncomfortable, messy, and awkward

---

44. Gibson and Mason, *Preaching Hope in Darkness,* 159.

45. Gibson and Mason, *Preaching Hope in Darkness,* 154.

46. Gibson and Mason, *Preaching Hope in Darkness,* 62.

topic. Perspectives on suicide may vary, even in one's congregation, from advocating that "A person who dies by suicide is headed to hell" to "Suicide is like any other death." We may think that to raise the topic of suicide may risk encouraging someone to go through with it. There may be concern about copycat deaths. Additionally, we have limited biblical information on suicide, but we do have a rich, textured understanding of the value of the person. Sometimes we're not sure about the ethical elements to suicide and its ramifications. We don't want to offend anyone, either. So, we don't talk about it. We don't preach about it. We remain silent. "When preachers don't address significant issues in some way, regardless of how controversial or difficult they may be," says Clemons, "one of two messages comes thundering through the silence: either preachers don't care or they don't know what to say."[47]

Pastors have a sacred task to address suicide from the pulpit to show suicidal congregants that the Bible and church are relevant to their lives. Chapter 3 in this book and *Preaching Hope in Darkness* will give you many concrete ideas for how to preach and teach about suicide safely.

Rhythms in the Life of the Church

The Lord's Supper

Some churches have very few rhythms and others have many. One rhythm in the life of the church might be the Lord's Supper or Eucharist. The importance of the Lord's Supper is reminding us of the covenant relationship we have with God. This covenant relationship is very important in the midst of suffering and is one of the themes in lament psalms. Lament psalms have a structure: Protest, Petition, Praise. The reason that lament psalms end with Praise is that suffering people remind themselves that they are in a covenant relationship with God which obligates God to be present in their suffering.[48] Psalm 13, a lament psalm, ends like this:

> But I trust in your unfailing love;
>
> my heart rejoices in your salvation.
>
> I will sing the LORD's praise,
>
> for he has been good to me.

---

47. Clemons, *Sermons on Suicide.*

48. Gibson and Mason, *Preaching Hope in Darkness*, 137.

When David says "unfailing love," he uses the word *chesed*, which is God's covenant love, God's unfailing love because it is love expressed in the context of a covenant. He hasn't yet seen God intervene in this situation, but David is obstinately depending on God. He trusts in God's covenant and character of love. In the future tense, David says that he will sing God's praise, because God has been good to him, or has dealt bountifully with him.[49] Christians don't engage in the Praise section in a flippant, careless way, and they don't engage in the Lord's Supper without being reminded of God's great covenant love for them. God took the shame of the cross by dying on it, and turned shame and what looked like defeat into the victory over our sin. His death looked like a hopeless dead-end situation to the disciples, but was followed by an unexpected triumph over death, the resurrection. Do we need any more proof that God can take hopeless circumstances and redeem them? The Praise section of lament psalms affirm that God is in the business of redeeming hopeless situations, those in the past and ours in the present. We affirm this covenant relationship every time we celebrate the Lord's Supper (Matt 26:26–29; Mark 14:22–25; Luke 22:14–20; 1 Cor 11:25). It is on the basis of our relationship with God that we petition him in the midst of suffering. The Lord's Supper can help remind us of the hope of the gospel. As Pastor Talitha says, "Worship connects us with this very powerful story that runs the gamut of the human experience and lets us know that God has not abandoned us."

More Rhythms of the Life of the Church

But it is not just the rhythm of the Lord's Supper that helps suffering people. It is the rhythm of the life of the church in a week, in a year and in a lifetime. This rhythm can be an anchor to life for a person thinking about suicide. As one of our study participants said, "[Churches' one-month focus] turns into a twelve-month application of caring for people in their faith community."[50]

- *The weekly rhythm.* Pastor Talitha says, "The rituals and structure of worship is an anchor in the week. It stops the 'hamster brain.' It gives me a day to think of something other than whatever it is that is 'hamstering around in my head.'" The commandment to observe Sabbath rest (Exod 20:8–11) emphasizes the importance of this anchor.

49. Bullock, *Psalms*, 91.

50. Unpublished interview from Mason et al., "How Counselors Can Help."

- *The annual rhythm.* Pastor Talitha points out, "There is a rhythm to the year. You go into Advent. It provides people a chance in the midst of all the falderal of Christmas to say, 'This is a story about nothing working out, of a couple having to leave their home, a baby born in a barn, nothing working out, but somehow God being present.' That can help prevent suicide. It lets people know they are not alone. The same thing is true with Lent. I hated Easter as an early adolescent because, with all the things going on in my family, when I didn't feel very resurrected. But once I started taking the Holy Week journey, I realized the story doesn't just go from Palm Sunday to Easter. Instead, you have to go through the deep valley in between. You have to hear the cry from the cross that says, 'Why have you abandoned me?' If you hear that, then Easter makes sense."

Rev. Dr. Sherry Molock, co-pastor of Beloved Community Church, explains their church's annual rhythms:

> During Suicide Prevention week, we have sermons and teachings about suicide. During July, it's national minority mental health awareness month. We talk about it in October, which is Suicide Awareness Month. So there is a sermon on it in October. We've had Bible studies on it, and Sunday School lessons on it.[51]

> Rev. Dr. Molock adds that this rhythm "normalizes" talking about mental health and suicide. She expressed the wish that more churches would participate in the National Weekend of Prayer to increase suicide prevention awareness. She wishes for "a more coordinated effort . . . to be more [suicide] prevention oriented" throughout a denomination.[52] Pastor Amy (from ch. 2) agrees on a year-round focus: "[Suicide is] being preached about, people are giving testimonies about it, we are praying about it. It's clear that we don't all have it all together. Everybody does this once a year." The annual rhythm infuses suicide prevention into the fabric of the church. As Pastor Talitha says, "[Conversations about mental health and suicide] are normalized in the life of the congregation."[53]

Another possible annual rhythm suggested by Dr. Melinda Moore (see ch. 7) is an annual depression screening day.[54] And it is important

---

51. Unpublished interview from Mason et al., "How Counselors Can Help."
52. Unpublished interview from Mason et al., "How Counselors Can Help."
53. Unpublished interview from Mason et al., "How Counselors Can Help."
54. Unpublished interview from Mason et al., "How Counselors Can Help."

to balance annual rhythms with a culture of suicide prevention. As one study participant cautions, one time annual events focused on suicide prevention can

> Inadvertently [make] people think [suicide] is an unusual problem. What [works better] is a culture in a church body, [modeled] by the leadership, of authenticity and vulnerability and social connectedness, and support. I'm not a fan of big events focused on suicide prevention, but just weaving it into the dialogue of how we do life, to say that [suffering] is a part of human struggle, and when it happens, we can turn to each other, and find others who are safe to help us through that.[55]

- *The rhythm of a lifetime.* Pastor Talitha explains,

  Worship gives us rituals for the stages and ages of life: baptism, confirmation and funerals, even a ritual around a divorce or the ritual of being with someone in a hospital, and the ritual of being a pastor and visiting a family where there has been a death by suicide.

  She suggests that these rituals can be an anchor for people. She suggests,

  > Use the funeral, use worship in general as a pastoral care, pastoral education time. . . . Worship, and especially congregational singing, runs the whole gamut of life, that gives voice to lament, to joy and everything else in between.

Pastor Talitha recommends Will Willimon's perspective that it is worship that edifies and nurtures a congregation into a vital faith and unity.[56] Worship is pastoral care because it heals, sustains, guides, and reconciles those committed to the pastor's care.[57] It forms and transforms the people in worship.[58] Pastor Talitha adds that worship is just one entry point for engaging congregants. Her church also offers congregants opportunities for service like volunteering with Habitat for Humanity.[59] She says, "Helping others also helps us find meaning and purpose, even in the hard times."

---

55. Unpublished interview from Mason et al., "How Counselors Can Help."

56. Willimon, *Worship as Pastoral Care*, 19.

57. Willimon, *Worship as Pastoral Care*, 48.

58. Willimon, *Worship as Pastoral Care*, 197.

59. Unpublished interview from Mason et al., "How Counselors Can Help."

In this chapter, we finished laying the foundation for suicide prevention in a church: a worshipping church. A church signals in their worship that they are ready to have conversations about suicide. However, a church also needs to be ready to help a suicidal person who reaches out for help. Suicide prevention consultant Fe writes,

> There is every indication that most suicides are preventable. However, prevention requires two things. People who are thinking about suicide must feel safe telling others, and people who suspect that someone else is thinking about suicide must feel comfortable asking them about it.[60]

If a suicidal person feels safe to reach out for help, the church needs to know how to help. In the next chapter, we move to building the frame of intervention. We will lay out a plan for how equip a church to help those who reach out for help.

Discussion Questions

1. What inaccurate beliefs have you discovered in worship songs?

2. Why do Christians suffer?

3. Would congregants in a liturgical faith tradition with more rhythms in the life of the church have more opportunity to feel connection to other congregants? Why or why not?

4. Do you feel a binding to fellow congregants during worship? Why or why not?

5. How else might worship help prevent suicide?

6. The writer of Hebrews 10:25 says, "Let us not neglect meeting together." Why is communal worship so important?

Take Stock of Your Church

1. What view of suffering does your church's worship imply?

2. Has the word "suicide" ever been mentioned in your church? Where and when?

---

60. Avis, *Second Day*, 114.

3. In what part of worship might it make sense to speak the word "suicide"?

4. How might suicidal people in your church react to hearing the word "suicide" said out loud in church? How might they react if the word "suicide" is never spoken?

Resources

National Action Alliance for Suicide Prevention Faith Communities Task Force Faith. Hope.Life National Weekend of Prayer. https://theactionalliance.org/faith-hope-life

World Suicide Prevention Day. https://www.who.int/news-room/events/detail/2019/09/10/default-calendar/world-suicide-prevention-day

Currie, David A. *The Big Idea of Biblical Worship: The Development and Leadership of Expository Services.* Peabody: Hendrickson, 2017.

Gibson, Scott, and Karen Mason. *Preaching Hope in Darkness: Help for Pastors in Addressing Suicide from the Pulpit.* Bellingham: Lexham, 2020.

Willimon, William H. *Worship as Pastoral Care.* Nashville: Abingdon, 1979.

988 Suicide & Crisis Lifeline. https://988lifeline.org/

Part 2: **Intervention**

CHAPTER 5

Essential Element 4: A Skilled, Equipped Church

Do not harm yourself! (Acts 16:28)

Do not withhold good from those to whom it is due,
when it is in your power to act.
Do not say to your neighbor,
"Come back tomorrow and I'll give it to you"—
when you already have it with you. (Prov 3:27–28)

REV. GLEN BLOOMSTROM[1] IS a retired US Army Chaplain who was assigned around the world to many combat deployments and staff assignments in the Pentagon. His goal was to model the gentle grace of God to others. He said,

> I have always had a heart to comfort others. Other chaplains got into their role as a warrior-chaplain. Even though I was an Airborne and Ranger Chaplain, I always saw myself as a safe person in units where I served, like an older brother or an uncle to those I served.

Glen first encountered suicide in the military and became interested in learning more about suicide when a soldier died by suicide. "It was really traumatic for me." He realized that the other soldiers in the unit were in shock. They experienced an overwhelming combination of rage, anger,

1. Author interview with Chaplain Glen Bloomstrom, February 2, 2021. Chaplain (Colonel, retired) Glen Bloomstrom, MDiv, MS, MSS, served thirty years as a US Army Chaplain. He is the LivingWorks Faith Program developer and director of faith community engagement for LivingWorks. He is a member of the Faith Communities Task Force, National Action Alliance for Suicide Prevention, and Adjunct Instructor of Pastoral Counseling at Bethlehem Seminary in Minneapolis, Minnesota.

shame, confusion and re-experienced traumas from their past. They asked, "We survived combat. How could this happen with such an elite and powerful group of soldiers? We are Rangers." Glen also lost a chaplain friend to suicide. "He had a brilliant mind, but he was deeply scarred by circumstances in his life. We spent a lot of time together, and he shared his suicidal thoughts with me and we got him help." However, one weekend, his friend killed himself. Other people asked, "How could a chaplain do this? How could *this* chaplain do this? He was so vibrant and full of life, such a wonderful preacher and teacher, a caring individual. People were just devastated by this." These experiences made Glen want to learn about the unique grief following a suicide and help other chaplains whom he knew to be "woefully unprepared" to deal with suicide.

At the Pentagon, when he was involved in policy development, he discovered the importance of *skills-based* and *evidence-based* programs for teaching chaplains how to prevent suicide. He realized that an evidence-based program, developed by professional suicidologists, was much more effective than an "in-house" training. He brought these convictions into retirement and applied them in the church and in the development of LivingWorks Faith.[2]

The first step in building the frame for suicide intervention is becoming a *skilled, equipped church*. Once a suicidal person feels safe enough to reach out for help, the church must know what to do. We'll see how a church can become equipped with a model of suicide intervention. We will also see that some churches provide easily accessible materials.

Why Is Not Being Skilled and Equipped a Problem?

Suicidal people reach out to pastors. Pastors are as likely to be contacted as mental health professionals.[3] People tend to view pastors as "first-line helpers" for most mental health problems, including suicidal behaviors.[4] In our many studies, pastors tell us that suicidal people reach out to them for help.[5] They describe being in positions of frontline caregivers

---

2. See the website: https://www.livingworks.net/faith.

3. Hohman and Larson, "Psychiatric Factors Predicting Use of Clergy"; Wang et al., "Patterns and Correlates of Contacting Clergy."

4. Ellison et al., "Clergy as a Source of Mental Health Assistance."

5. Mason et al., "Clergy Referral of Suicidal Individuals."

for suicidal people in their congregations and communities. For example, one pastor said,

> Within the first week of my being [at my first church], a woman called me, said she was sitting at her home and she had a razor blade beside her, and she didn't see any reason to live anymore, and that was, like, day two or three on the job.[6]

Pastors say they are contacted on average by at least one suicidal person per year, with an average of two contacts per year.[7] And even though many pastors believe that they are being proactive in preparing to minister to those at risk of suicide,[8] a quarter to a third of pastors say they have no training.[9]

But it's not just pastors. As we saw in the Introduction, a suicidal friend from church reached out to me before I was trained as a psychologist. Suicidal people will reach out to congregants, too. Former Pastor Fe Anam Avis (from ch. 8) is convinced that the whole church must be ready to help a suicidal congregant. Just as Paul noticed that the Philippian jailer was getting ready to kill himself, and just as Paul gave him a reason to live, the church must recognize the suicidal congregant and then intervene. This is what Fe writes:

> We must see the person at risk. . . . [Church] members should be equipped to become comfortable asking people if they are thinking about suicide. . . . We must be clear about our role. Church members are not being called to become amateur therapists. . . . Suicidal behavior can often be prevented through the call of a persistent and loving voice. This saving act is possible for anyone and appropriate to a body that lays claim to the priesthood of all believers.[10]

The problem is that pastors and congregants are undertrained.[11] One pastor told us, "[Suicide] is the biggest area that I was sort of clueless on when

---

6. Mason et al., "Clergy Referral of Suicidal Individuals," 4.

7. Mason et al., "Clergy as Suicide Prevention Gatekeepers"; Mason et al., "Clergy Use of Suicide Prevention Competencies."

8. Smietana, "1 in 3 Protestant Churchgoers Personally Affected by Suicide."

9. Mason et al., "Clergy as Suicide Prevention Gatekeepers"; Mason et al., "Clergy Use of Suicide Prevention Competencies."

10. Avis, *Second Day*, 112–14.

11. Marshall, "Clergy Workgroup."

I went into the ministry."[12] Another told us that ministering to a suicidal person makes him "scared spitless."[13] Another said,

> The counseling courses I took for my MDiv were entirely, without doubt, lacking any substance, actual training, or real merit. We were told to refer. That's all. And while I agree that I am not trained to serve as someone's therapist or psychiatrist, I am, all too often, the first person they come to when fighting depression or suicide. I needed and still need basic counseling techniques to have been taught. I learned much of that working at a domestic violence shelter where I dealt with suicidal individuals often. But that came from experience, not training. In addition, formal theological training addressing these issues that did more than battle over whether or not suicide is a sin (how helpful is that going to be in that moment?) would have been of great value the first time someone walked into my office and asked if their mom was in hell because of her suicide.[14]

Pastor Amy (from ch. 2) said, "When the suicidal gentleman came to me as a pastor, I felt terribly ill-equipped."

Pastors receive a lot more training in counseling in general and receive much less training in helping suicidal people.[15] In one of our studies, we found that pastors were missing key knowledge such as the higher suicide rates among middle-aged men.[16] We also found that pastors do better at estimating suicide risk and intervening when they have more knowledge about suicide and when the risk is high, but not when the risk is less obvious.[17] Most clergy we talk to say they need more suicide-related training.[18]

But pastors enlist the help of the whole church in ministering to suicidal people. One pastor said, "It isn't just me trying to help this [suicidal] person, it is the church's ministry."[19] Congregants also need to be prepared to help. Pastor Amy says, "One stigma is suicide is for the professionals to deal with. I think it's much more likely that the person who needs help will send a signal to someone around them." She advises the need to train "the

12. Mason et al., "Clergy Referral of Suicidal Individuals," 5.

13. Mason et al., "Developmental Model."

14. Mason et al., "Clergy as Suicide Prevention Gatekeepers."

15. Mason et al., "Clergy as Suicide Prevention Gatekeepers."

16. Mason et al., "Clergy as Suicide Prevention Gatekeepers."

17. Mason et al., "Clergy as Suicide Prevention Gatekeepers."

18. Mason et al., "Clergy as Suicide Prevention Gatekeepers," 87.

19. Mason et al., "Clergy Referral of Suicidal Individuals," 6.

everyday person" so they can ask, "Are you thinking about suicide?" She adds, "Asking is so important. Then after you ask, just sitting and listening to them name that they have had thoughts of suicide." A pastor in one of our studies emphasized the listening,

> It is not our job to heap anything else on them other than the grace of God for them and the love of Christ for them where they are. It is coming alongside them, listening, loving them, assuring them that whatever drove them to that point, the Lord knows, and he is not angry with them. And how can we as a community of faith just come alongside them and do whatever it takes.[20]

It is important to know that asking about suicide does not plant the idea in the mind of the suicidal person or create distress.[21] Being asked about suicidal thinking can be a relief for the suicidal person. They were never taught by their parents or teachers what to do with these thoughts. They are looking for someone to listen to them. Pastor Amy shared this picture,

> Having thoughts of suicide is like having a great big balloon blown up behind them. [For this person] having someone ask them the question [about their suicidal thinking] was like someone gently letting some of the air out of the balloon. Just having someone ask just takes the pressure away. And it's just like a huge relief. When it does happen, . . . it just has a calming effect and it takes the power away from suicide. But people don't ask.

As a pastor in another study explained, "Most people would like to come alongside those who are hurting. They just don't know what to do."[22]

What Do We Know about a Skilled, Equipped Church?

We have found in our research that pastors need a lot of different skills to help a suicidal person and that these skills develop over time and with practice.[23] They need to know their role as the spiritual leader in a suicidal situation, but they also need to know mental health basics. They need to

---

20. Unpublished interview from Mason et al., "How Counselors Can Help."

21. Harris and Goh, "Is Suicide Assessment Harmful to Participants?"; Law et al., "Does Assessing Suicidality Frequently and Repeatedly Cause Harm?"; Eynan et al., "Effects of Suicide Ideation Assessments"; Gould et al., "Evaluating Iatrogenic Risk."

22. Unpublished interview from Mason et al., "How Counselors Can Help."

23. Mason et al., "Developmental Model."

listen instead of finding a quick solution. They develop confidence to walk with the suicidal person with the humility of, "I don't have all the answers." They get trained to evaluate how risky the situation is and how to plan for safety. They refer because they don't want to overstep their role or their competencies. They work to balance caring for their family and themselves with helping others. They work to foster a church community where everyone watches over each other: "We are a community that takes care of each other."[24] Pastors tend to rely on their counseling skills when they don't have these skills.[25] They use more suicide-specific competencies when they have more suicide training hours.[26] In this chapter we'll see how to get training in a "best practice,"[27] a recognized best approach for how to help a suicidal person who seeks your help, and how to train an entire church.

How Do We Develop a Skilled, Equipped Church?

How does a church become a skilled, equipped church which helps suicidal people who reach out? One of the first steps, according to Chaplain Glen, is having conversations with leadership. Church leaders need to see suicide prevention as part of their role in caring for congregants. They also need to be ready to take action because it is likely they will be contacted by a suicidal person at some point in their ministry. Chaplain Glen suggests presenting a theologically-informed approach to church leadership. Discuss biblical references to suicide such as the Apostle Paul telling the Philippian Jailer, "Don't harm yourself!" (Acts 16:28), and the Apostle Paul who said "We despaired of life itself" (2 Cor 1:8). Such passages connect Scripture to the human experience of desperation and suicide.[28] Fe provides the following theologically-informed approach:

> What is your theology of [the fruit of the Spirit]? My theology is that the Spirit gives us the motivation for [love, joy, peace, etc.], but we need to be equipped in those. When Paul prays that we need to abound in knowledge and insight: And this is my prayer:

24. Mason et al., "Developmental Model."

25. Mason et al., "Clergy Use of Suicide Prevention Competencies."

26. Mason et al., "Clergy Use of Suicide Prevention Competencies."

27. World Health Organization, *Preventing Suicide*, 38.

28. At least six suicide deaths are described in the Bible: Abimelech (Judg 9:52-54), Samson (Judg 16:30), Saul and his armor bearer (1 Sam 31:4), Ahithophel (2 Sam 17:23), Zimri (1 Kgs 16:18), and Judas (Matt 27:5; Acts 1:18).

> that your love may abound more and more in knowledge and depth of insight (Phil 1:9), love itself as a motivation is essential, but it's not complete unless there is additional equipping. It doesn't abound. You don't want the person doing your open heart surgery saying, "I have no training, but I love you." I have a theology of the gift of the Spirit that requires [people] to be equipped, not just motivated. In addition to having these conversations, we need people to be able to do interventions.

To help leadership understand the importance of being a skilled, equipped church, Chaplain Glen adds that having helpers tell their story of what it's like to be trained and untrained can be helpful. "I felt so ill-equipped." "I didn't know what to do." "I didn't know how to advise parents." "I am afraid I'll say the wrong thing." LivingWorks Faith begins with faith leaders telling their stories of what it felt like to be ill-equipped.

After leadership understands the importance of becoming skilled and equipped, Chaplain Glen suggests finding a training that is faith-specific. People of faith want to hear about suicide prevention from their own theological perspective. LivingWorks Faith is that kind of training. LivingWorks Faith's goal is to reduce fear and anxiety around suicide prevention and to save lives, with biblical wisdom integrated throughout the training.

Chaplain Glen emphasizes the importance of selecting a training that is skills-based and evidence-based. By a skills-based training, he means a training that allows practicing each skill, a training focused on practical skills that can be applied and used. By evidence-based, he means a training with research evidence about the training's effectiveness, evidence that the training actually increases skill level and saves lives.

Most clergy we have interviewed mention the following suicide intervention programs: be nice.Faith,[29] CAMS,[30] or Chaplains-CARE,[31] the Connect Program,[32] LivingWorks,[33] the QPR Institute,[34] RemedyLIVE,[35] or

---

29. https://www.benice.org/.

30. https://cams-care.com/.

31. https://millifelearning.militaryonesource.mil/.

32. http://www.theconnectprogram.org/.

33. https://www.livingworks.net/.

34. https://www.qprinstitute.com/.

35. https://www.remedylive.com/.

Soul Shop.[36] Some churches get trained in a mental health ministry that includes a unit on suicide prevention.[37]

After selecting the training, Pastor Amy emphasizes the benefit of asking an outside trainer to come in to model the vulnerability that is so important in fostering "deep community"[38] in a church:

> If a pastor or a church leader brings someone in [to train], that models "I'm not an expert in everything. I need to reach out and get support and help. We as a community need to reach out and bring in someone who has experience around suicide to help us learn how to talk about it." I think it's good modelling for reaching out for help.

Finally, Chaplain Glen suggests that each church develop a *network of safety*, a type of pyramid where many are trained to recognize a suicidal congregant and a few are trained as "gatekeepers," people with more training. Pastor Jim Liske likens a gatekeeper to a lifeguard. He wants "pastors [to] understand, 'You don't have to be the mental health professional. You just need to be the lifeguard. Your church can be trained to get people out of the water onto the beach and to call the paramedic.'"[39] Chaplain Glen agrees, "Once a person is identified as suicidal, they can be 'referred up' [to the gatekeeper]." Chaplain Glen offers this example of a network of safety, using the LivingWorks trainings (which include LivingWorks Start [ninety minutes online], safeTALK [four hours in person], LivingWorks Faith [five–six hours online], LivingWorks ASIST [two days in person], and Suicide to Hope [one day]):

1. All interested church members would complete LivingWorks Start to learn to identify suicidal people in the congregation.

2. Natural helpers and volunteers would complete safeTALK to learn to recognize when someone needs help and connect them to a gatekeeper. These volunteers are naturally collaborative listeners.

---

36. See webesite: https://www.soulshopmovement.org/.

37. See webesite: Mental Health Gateway, https://mentalhealthgateway.org/; Interfaith Network on Mental Illness, http://inmi.us/; Mental Health First Aid, https://www.mentalhealthfirstaid.org/; NAMI Faith Net, https://www.nami.org/Get-Involved/NAMI-FaithNet; United Church of Christ Mental Health Network, https://www.mhn-ucc.org/.

38. Unpublished interview from Mason et al., "How Counselors Can Help."

39. Unpublished interview from Mason et al., "How Counselors Can Help."

3. Associate Ministry Leaders would complete LivingWorks Faith and Living Works ASIST to become gatekeepers and foster a culture of transparency.

4. A Senior Ministry Leader would complete LivingWorks Faith and Living Works ASIST to become a gatekeeper and establish a culture of hope, openness and support.

5. A person who has lived experience with suicidal thoughts, and possible recurring thoughts of suicide, would complete Suicide to Hope to learn from past experiences and stay safe if those thoughts return.

Chaplain Glen explains that an advantage of a network-of-safety approach is that everyone in church will "speak the same language." Chaplain Glen says this network of safety is characterized by "people watching over and caring for each other with skills and confidence to address mental health and suicide." He adds that a church can develop protocols or official procedures for how to refer a suicidal person up the pyramid toward a gatekeeper. He also points out that the network of safety can include ministries that already exist, like Celebrate Recovery. Chaplain Glen also suggests that a church can start with a small network of safety and expand it over time. Fe has the same vision:

> For every hundred [congregants], we need a pastor or someone trained in ASIST.[40] Not everyone is called to be trained in ASIST. A few people are. You have to stratify it. You have to figure out, what do we want people to be able to do? Not everyone is called to do all those things but we're all called to some level of basic competency.

Chaplain Glen suggests that such a network of safety can be expanded into the community. Trainees can bring their skills to their neighborhoods. One of our study participants pointed out that inviting the community to a training is "a great opportunity to share the love of Christ."[41] Chaplain Glen is convinced that "the community welcomes the church being better equipped because that knits the community together and creates a stronger coalition (crisis lines, health centers, mental health counselors, hospitals, schools . . .)."

An advantage of including the community is that this type of cooperation can help pay for trainings. Pastor Amy found funding sources in her

40. ASIST is Applied Suicide Intervention Skills Training: https://www.livingworks.net/asist.

41. Unpublished interview from Mason et al., "How Counselors Can Help."

community to cover the expenses of bringing in trainings for her community after a sixth grader in the neighboring community had died by suicide. She arranged for an entire community, including faith communities and schools, to get trained. She says,

> Churches can pool together. There are finances out there. . . . Every church and every community has people who have big hearts for the community and finding those resources in a community to come together to help with the funding and help with getting the word out. . . . There needs to be a lot more networking in communities.

Accessible Materials

One way to get started with intervention is to provide accessible materials on suicide prevention to the congregation. Many pastors have told us that accessible materials signal that the church is a safe place to discuss suicide. Rev. Dr. Sherry Molock, co-pastor of Beloved Community Church with her husband, Rev. Guy Molock Jr., has said,

> We have materials in our sanctuary that we pass out all the time, and also some brochures in the back room in case people don't feel comfortable picking them up on the community table. We have the hotline number on our website and Facebook page, and we have the [988 Suicide & Crisis Lifeline] number on our website and Facebook page, and . . . in our announcement slide.[42]

They also have the [988 Suicide & Crisis] Lifeline magnet in the bathroom and in the bulletin, which a congregant can bring home. Dr. Melinda Moore's church includes suicide prevention information in the church bulletin during the National Weekend of Prayer. Her bishop encourages all the churches in the diocese to do the same. Many excellent materials can be found on websites like the American Foundation for Suicide Prevention, the American Association of Suicidology, the 988 Suicide & Crisis Lifeline, and the Suicide Prevention Resource Center. Pastor Amy cautions that though these organizations have excellent resources, "The only thing that is not there is the faith questions. That's one of the pieces that churches should develop and have available."

Another equipping the Molocks have implemented at their church is helping families navigate the mental health system. They had congregants

42. Mason et al., "How Counselors Can Help."

bring their insurance cards to church and helped them understand their benefits.

Caring Letters

One last example of intervention is to equip congregants with a tool for what to do when they notice when another congregant stops coming to church. Rev. Dr. Sherry Molock encourages her congregants, "If you haven't seen someone in a while, give them a call."[43] Or send them a note. Pastor Amy has seen the power of a "card ministry."[44] Sending a letter can prevent suicide. Dr. Jerome Motto,[45] a psychiatrist, studied 3,006 patients who were discharged following a psychiatric hospital stay for depression or suicidal behaviors. He followed three groups:

1. Group 1 followed through with post-hospital-treatment,

2. Group 2 refused treatment; they received a non-demanding letter or phone calls on a set schedule, and

3. Group 3 refused treatment; they did not receive letters or calls.

He sent Group 2 letters or called them. Dr. Motto's letter said, "Dear X, It has been some time since you were here at the hospital and we hope things are going well for you. If you wish to drop us a note, we would be glad to hear from you." A self-addressed unstamped envelope was enclosed, and if the person wrote back, their letter was answered. Group 1 had the highest rates of suicide death, next Group 3, and last Group 2. A caring letter can help prevent suicide. A church can send caring letters or call or send a caring text.[46]

In this chapter, we started building the frame for suicide intervention. We saw how each person in a church can become skilled and equipped to help a suicidal person who reaches out for help. We also saw how some churches use easily-accessible materials or send caring letters. In the next chapter, we'll finish building the frame for intervention by showing how to connect with community resources.

---

43. Unpublished interview from Mason et al., "How Counselors Can Help."

44. Unpublished interview from Mason et al., "How Counselors Can Help."

45. Motto, "Suicide Prevention for High-Risk Persons"; Motto and Bostrom, "Post-crisis Suicide Prevention."

46. Comtois et al., "Effect of Augmenting Standard Care."

Discussion Questions

1. If you became suicidal, what would you do?

2. Who would you reach out to?

3. What would be most helpful to you?

Take Stock of Your Church

1. Which of your church leaders would need to support your church becoming a "skilled, equipped church"?

2. What is the theological context of your church? For example, is your church focused on evangelism and would need to see suicide prevention as a ministry to unchurched people?

3. How would you select a suicide intervention training program?

4. How would your church develop a "network of safety" (pyramid of trained people)?

5. Who in your church are natural helpers? Volunteers?

6. If your church has a mental health ministry, how would you include a suicide prevention component in the mental health ministry?

Resources

Trainings

be nice.Faith. https://www.benice.org/our-programs/faith
CAMS (Collaborative Assessment and Management of Suicidality). https://cams-care.com/about-cams/
Chaplains-CARE. https://millifelearning.militaryonesource.mil/
Connect Program. https://theconnectprogram.org/
LivingWorks Faith. https://www.livingworks.net/faith
LivingWorks Faith Networks of Safety. https://www.youtube.com/watch?v=bHapWrTq1ss https://www.youtube.com/watch?v=2Dj89yObt-0
QPR for clergy. https://courses.qprinstitute.com/index.php
RemedyLIVE. https://www.remedylive.com/
Soul Shop. https://www.soulshopmovement.org/

Other Resources

American Foundation for Suicide Prevention. https://afsp.org/
American Association of Suicidology. https://suicidology.org/
Mason, Karen. *Preventing Suicide: A Handbook for Clergy, Chaplains and Pastoral Counselors.* Downers Grove: InterVarsity, 2014.
National Action Alliance for Suicide Prevention. https://theactionalliance.org/
988 Suicide & Crisis Lifeline. https://988lifeline.org/
Suicide Prevention Resource Center. https://sprc.org/

CHAPTER 6

Essential Element 5: A Well-Networked Church

Seek the shalom of the city where I have caused you to be carried away captive, and pray to the LORD for it; for in the shalom of it shall you have shalom. (Jer 29:7)

DR. BISHOP C. GUY Robinson says that he "stumbled" onto his passion for mental health and the church. He took psychology of religion courses, saw the needs in his church, and then developed his interest into a passion. He says, "I'm no Moses, but I stumbled onto that burning bush."

Bishop Robinson began his ministry as a composer and musician before being called to the pastorate. He compares his passion for mental health with his passion for music: "I started being musical by ear and then my dad made me go to school for it. I started to be able to put the nomenclature of the discipline to the experiences which I took to naturally." The same thing happened to his passion for mental health in the church. He had a natural interest in psychology of religion and parlayed his interest into a doctor of ministry in marriage and family. His realizations about the importance of mental health in the church came to him experientially and through reading. He calls himself "a book nerd." Bishop Robinson remembers reading Roberts C. Roberts, who wrote that the Bible is not a book of systematic psychology any more than it is a book of systematic theology. However, a systematic psychology can be developed. Bishop Robinson said, "So I started paying attention. Paul is educated in Greco-Roman philosophical tradition and I see how often he talks about the mind. That became my passion."

After reflecting theologically and psychologically, Bishop Robinson presented to a breakout group during a convention. He presented first to a small classroom of pastors in his fellowship. Each year, by word of mouth, his audience grew. He now presents to larger groups, at pastor conferences through the year and around the US. When he first started, "there was no other preacher with a mental health hermeneutic." He has seen the interest in mental health grow exponentially.

In addition to his pastoral role, Bishop Robinson is forming a team of African American mental health professionals. He and the team are working to address the stigma of mental health and the mistrust that people may have of the system. They are developing a program to provide a nomenclature about mental health that is *culturally aware and sensitive.* Bishop Robinson has found the importance of contextualizing based on the needs of his community. For example, in his urban Baltimore context, parishioners can stigmatize mental health conditions as "cracking under the pressures" of societal inequities as well as a failure of faith. Bishop Robinson has found that he needs to know the needs of his community in order to meet his parishioners where they are. He says, "We have to meet people in their place of need." Knowing his community is key to creating a well-networked church. Keep reading to find out how Dr. Bishop C. Guy Robinson developed a mental health ministry in his denomination and developed a well-networked church in his community.[1]

In this chapter, we will finish building the frame for suicide intervention. We will see why it is crucial for a church to be a *well-networked church* connected to community resources, and how to do that.

What Are the Challenges to Becoming Well-Networked?

One challenge to being well-networked is that churches must learn about resources in their community before they can refer to them. Resources include people like mental health providers and services like hospitals or food pantries or temporary shelter. Most suicidal people need these types of resources because they have at least some symptoms of a mental health

---

1. Author interview with Dr. Bishop C. Guy Robinson, February 4, 2021. Robinson is pastor of the Tabernacle of the Lord Church and Ministries in Baltimore, Maryland. He serves as State Bishop of Maryland for the Full Gospel Baptist Church Fellowship. He holds a BA from Morgan State University in clinical pastoral education, an MDiv from Howard University, and a DMin in marriage and family from Gordon-Conwell Theological Seminary.

condition,[2] but they also have aspects of their lives that "are not working for them."[3]

Suicide prevention consultant Fe (see ch. 8) recommends thinking broadly about needed community resources. He advocates

> an intentional effort to develop a network to access the wide range of resources needed to reduce suicidal desperation, i.e. domestic violence, legal, employment, housing, counseling, drug and alcohol services, etc. People only think about the mental illness side of suicide prevention. But churches need to think about the broader picture of what people need in order to help them want to live and not die. And that is holistic. It's spiritual, economic, all of these kinds of things. If the church is going to be effective at helping people deal with suicide along with a number of other things, a church will need a network of resources.

Developing this network of resources is challenging because needs are great. A study participant said "In a multi-ethnic community, the need for resources is so great."[4] But resources are sometimes hidden. Churches learn about resources by word of mouth or through experience. Pastors try to refer to professionals they know, based on "established trusting relationship,"[5] but forming those relationships takes time. One pastor in one of our studies captured how awful it is to be without resources, "It's more that lack of resources, known to me, that is just about the scariest thing that I face."[6] Add to this challenge that resources come in all shapes and sizes, and knowing which suicidal congregant will be a good fit with which resource is often speculation. As a psychologist, an insider in the profession, I can't predict a good match between a client and a mental health provider.

Another challenge to becoming well-networked is the "fragmented mental health service delivery system."[7] One example is that some insurance plans limit their coverage of mental health services though fair

---

2. Kessler et al., "Trends in Suicide Ideation"; Harris and Barraclough, "Suicide as an Outcome"; Joiner et al., *The Interpersonal Theory of Suicide*, 21, 44. In some studies, up to 54 percent of suicide fatalities did not have a mental health condition (Centers for Disease Control and Prevention, *Vitalsigns*).

3. Mason et al., "How Counselors Can Help."

4. Unpublished interview from Mason et al., "How Counselors Can Help."

5. McMinn et al., "Basic and Advanced Competence."

6. Mason et al., "Clergy Referral of Suicidal Individuals," 6.

7. New Freedom Commission on Mental Health, *Achieving the Promise.*

insurance coverage is the law.[8] Another example is the disparities of availability of mental health resources in certain communities.[9]

A last challenge with being well-networked is that some pastors do not see themselves as frontline mental health workers.[10] Some pastors don't see themselves as part of the team that addresses the mental health needs to their congregants. However, pastors do provide pastoral counseling and make about seven referrals to mental health providers per year.[11] Making a referral means directing congregants to the right resources, based on the pastor's assessment of their needs.[12]

Seven referrals per year is fewer than would be expected. There might be a few reasons for this. Early in their careers, pastors might be a "quivering mass of availability"[13] and do not refer. They overextend themselves in terms of doing more than they are trained to do. It is not until they begin to grow in their pastoral role that they begin to know the boundaries of their competence and begin to develop collaborative relationships with other professionals. Later, they know when the situation merits seeking outside help and know that referral and follow-up are needed. They know how to continue to provide spiritual care even when their congregant may get help from other providers. What this means is that referral is a skill that pastors develop through experience. It is a skill that benefits pastors in the long run because referral helps them spread out the burden of caring for congregants with mental health conditions. Spreading out the burden is called "burden reduction," and it helps pastors care for themselves and their congregants.[14]

A difficulty with referrals for suicidal congregants is that churches often think first about hospitalization as the best referral. However, hospitalization is not guaranteed to lower suicide risk. About 3 to 10 percent of suicide deaths in the US occur during hospitalization.[15] One research team in England and Wales studied 2,177 suicides and found 358 (16 percent)

---

8. Use www.parityregistry.com to register denials for mental health services.

9. Mason et al., "Clergy Referral of Suicidal Individuals," 6.

10. Farrell and Goebert, "Collaboration between Psychiatrists and Clergy."

11. Mason et al., "Clergy as Suicide Prevention Gatekeepers."

12. Mason et al., "Moral Deliberations."

13. Mason et al., "Developmental Model."

14. Milstein et al., "Implementation of a Program to Improve the Continuity of Mental Health Care," 220.

15. Joiner et al., *Interpersonal Theory of Suicide*, 88.

were psychiatric inpatients at the time of death, 21 percent of whom were under special observation in the hospital.[16] They also found that risk of suicide increases after a hospitalization. Five hundred nineteen (24 percent) suicides occurred within three months of hospital discharge, the highest number occurring in the first week after discharge. Most people who died by suicide were thought to have been at no or low immediate risk at the final contact at the hospital.[17] Another research team followed 3,690 people who had been hospitalized for a suicide attempt and found that the risk of re-attempt remained high for ten years, but the risk is greatest in the first two years following discharge.[18]

Another tricky aspect of referrals is that many people do not follow through on referrals. In one study of 55,302 people in twenty-one countries, about half of suicide attempt survivors were not in treatment. The most important reason for not seeking help was low perceived need (58 percent), followed by attitudes like the wish to handle the problem alone (40 percent), and barriers like financial concerns (15 percent).[19] Given the resistance that some congregants might have to a referral, pastors have told us[20] they encourage congregants to follow-up on referrals by saying "There's all kinds of help. . . . They are ready to help you in any way they can." Or "There are people out there that are there to help. And there are organizations that are out there to help her." But some congregants remain resistant. One pastor told us,

> You have another group, whether they are classical Pentecostal, which is a different breed, or whether they are embedded in the Black community, which is not quick to access mental health . . . how do you get these people to feel that going to a mental health professional is like going to your physical physician?[21]

16. Appleby et al., "Suicide within 12 Months."

17. Appleby et al., "Suicide within 12 Months."

18. Gibb et al., "Mortality and Further Suicidal Behavior."

19. Bruffaerts et al., "Treatment of Suicidal People."

20. Mason et al., "Moral Deliberations."

21. Mason et al., "Clergy Referral of Suicidal Individuals," 6.

How Do We Create a Well-Networked Church?

While challenging, the advantage of a well-networked church is having access to resources to help a suicidal congregant who probably has at least some symptoms of a mental health condition[22] and some aspects of their lives that "are not working for them."[23] How do churches do this?

The first step is that the leadership must support serving the needs of the congregation through networking in the community. Dr. Bishop C. Guy Robinson had the support of his presiding bishop, Bishop Joseph W. Walker III. However, he has had to continue to make the case for serving the mental health needs of his congregation. He has cautioned his leadership,

> If we don't meet this [mental health] need, this need will be met in other ways. If we don't create ministry that does it, and put it in the context of ministry, in an increasingly secular society, then we may raise a generation that goes to brunch, sees their therapist, and never comes in our sanctuaries.

Some churches see meeting the mental health needs of a community as an evangelistic outreach. Many study participants have told us that serving mental health needs is the mission field of the twenty-first century. One said, "Mental illness is one of the low-hanging fruit which obviously leads you to suicide prevention."[24] Another said that not addressing the mental health concerns of congregants is "missing the greatest evangelistic opportunity in the twenty-first century. . . . Suicide is a great open door."[25]

Rev. Dr. Dennis Goff of the Lutheran Foundation in Fort Wayne, Indiana says, "One of the ways you connect with people in the community is meet some of their needs and start talking about things [like mental health] that people in the community are dealing with."[26] He gives the example of a church in his area which provides weekly "Assistance Hours" to community members, to help community members navigate local resources and connect to them. He says, "It's a creative way of church addressing people's

---

22. Kessler et al., "Trends in Suicide Ideation"; Harris and Barraclough, "Suicide as an Outcome"; Joiner et al., *Interpersonal Theory of Suicide,* 21, 44. In some studies, up to 54 percent of suicide fatalities did not have a mental health condition (Centers for Disease Control and Prevention, *Vitalsigns*).

23. Mason et al., "How Counselors Can Help."

24. Mason et al., "How Counselors Can Help."

25. Unpublished interview from Mason et al., "How Counselors Can Help."

26. Unpublished interview from Mason et al., "How Counselors Can Help."

realistic needs in the community and most of those who come for assistance are not people that would show up on a Sunday morning."[27] Another study participant said that this approach positions the church "as the front door" for people to get the help they need and to connect to the church.[28]

After leadership supports networking with the community, broach the subject of mental health and address the theological concerns. Bishop Robinson cautions, "You have to start theologically. You have to start with the Bible. *Sola Scriptura*. You have to develop a mental health hermeneutic." There has to be a recognition that "spiritual concerns can sometimes present as mental health crises." Bishop Robinson presents Scriptures that address mental health, like Adam and Eve who experienced shame and the disruption of the family, and Psalm 43, which outlines the symptoms of depression. He helps pastors embrace the fact that "spiritual concerns can sometimes present as mental health crises."

Bishop Robinson teaches pastors how to think about mental health crises theologically. He educates them on misunderstandings, like "What does [mental health] have to do with church?" or, "We don't need [treatment]? We have faith!" or, "If you need [mental health treatment], your spiritual strength has somehow been compromised." He has addressed the fear that psychology will corrupt a Christian's spiritual walk. He has found that these misunderstandings must be addressed and resolved.

It is then important to teach pastors and congregants how to recognize a mental health or suicide crisis and to refer. Pastor Amy (from ch. 2) knows this type of training is vital. She says,

> Not a lot of continuing education tends to be around pastoral care. There's continuing education around writing sermons and how to do stewardship or how to do youth programs. But there's not a lot on how to address issues in pastoral counseling. There's good teaching that pastors should be sending people to professionals, but pastors need to learn more about acute suicidal thinking and other urgent mental health issues.

A part of this training is to help pastors see themselves as first responders and triage specialists. Bishop Robinson says, "In most cases, particularly true in the urban African American context, you are the closest thing to a mental health professional your parishioner will ever encounter." Pastor Amy adds, "The church is the ER that then sends people to the specialty they need."

27. Unpublished interview from Mason et al., "How Counselors Can Help."

28. Unpublished interview from Mason et al., "How Counselors Can Help."

What may be helpful for pastors to know is that referring to other services is not a hand off. Each professional is an essential member of a team. Pastors provide spiritual leadership in partnership with other resources.[29] Pastors have told us that it's important to stay involved. One pastor we interviewed said, "My job is sort of triage. Get in there, figure out what's going on, and connect them with the right people. . . . And then my role as pastor is to monitor that."[30] Pastor Amy suggests how to monitor the referral:

> There are little things that pastors can do to help the referral. They are small things, but the impact can be huge. . . . For example, the pastor could offer the suicidal person to come to the church to make those initial calls to maintain privacy. The pastor can follow up after the first session and can encourage them to attend at least three sessions. Pastors need to know that it can take a while to find the right counselor. With follow-up, the person doesn't have to share confidential information with the pastor. But the pastor can ask, "How did that go for you?" "Were you able to make a first appointment?" "How did the first appointment go?" "Have you been able to make your therapist appointments?" "What's it like for you to go?" "I'm really glad you're going. I really want to encourage you."

Next, widen the circle. Pastors train lay leaders, because as Pastor Amy says, "The pastor should never do that alone." Bishop Robinson says the pastor leads the congregation by example. The congregation learns by watching the pastor lead in "the fish bowl." Indirectly, a congregation can learn from their pastor about the importance of addressing mental health conditions, suicidal behaviors, and utilizing community resources.

An important part of the training, Bishop Robinson recommends, is to contextualize your approach with cultural awareness and sensitivity. Pastors and congregants must understand the needs of the community, the mistrust in systems and structures, or misunderstandings about mental health. The pastor must find the gaps and bridge them. In the urban African American context where Bishop Robinson ministers, the community needs are the stressors of disparities caused by racism.

> That is a reality and when parishioners come to me, that's where I have to develop my theodicy. Explanations for the presence of evil in the light of a good God are usually connected to the societal

29. Mason et al., "Developmental Model."
30. Mason et al., "Moral Deliberations."

> context. . . . African American theology sees systemic issues as the
> most immediate threat to flourishing in the Gospel of the King-
> dom, whereas our counterparts tend to see secularization as the
> most imminent threat. In the African American context, how can
> you not talk about eight minutes and forty-six seconds of a knee
> on a neck. You have to, if you're going to meet them at the point of
> their need, you have to meet them where they're hurting. You can't
> skirt over it or dismiss it. That's the place where they are hurting.

Bishop Robinson cautions pastors that they need to know the needs of the community in order to develop a mental health ministry. Rev. Dr. Sherry Molock adds that in predominately African American churches, "suicide is even more stigmatized."[31] Pastor Amy emphasizes that discrimination and disparities can be drivers for suicidal desperation in African American young men and that US society needs to take responsibility for creating "communities where people [would] rather die."[32]

Finally, it is important that churches develop relationships with community resources. Bishop Robinson advises, "It is not just a list of community helpers; it is relationships." He has found that "developing relationships reduces pastoral angst, their care and concern for their parishioners. Pastors will want to meet the mental health professionals who will influence their parishioners." Most people want to refer based on "established trusting relationships."[33]

To begin a list of community helpers, a pastor can consult with pastor colleagues. (Bishop Robinson reached out to his Continuing Pastoral Education [CPE] chaplain supervisor.) But churches could also cold call or find mental health professionals in their church, keeping some things in mind about mental health professionals. Bishop Robinson found,

> What might surprise pastors is that they will have to be the ones
> to reach out. That is a distinction between the pastoral call and the
> mental health call. Mental health professionals don't tend to reach
> out, while the pastor has a mandate to leave the ninety-nine and
> go after the one. The pastor needs to take that initial step to reach
> out to mental health professionals.

Bishop Robinson cautions that cold callers have to be ready to experience rejections. This was his cold call script: "I'm calling to foster relationships

31. Unpublished interview from Mason et al., "How Counselors Can Help."

32. Unpublished interview from Mason et al., "How Counselors Can Help."

33. McMinn et al., "Basic and Advanced Competence."

to find out how I can be a pipeline." Some mental health professionals would not understand his request. Bishop Robinson advises developing resilience to find the one "yes" in the midst of nine "nos." He says, "Reaching out is hard. You have to see it as your passion, as an extension of your pastoral ministry. Getting people to the *right* resources is the motivation." He has found that congregants will be more amenable to referrals if the pastor can say, "I know this person."

Pastor Amy acknowledges, "It takes a while to find those links." This is what she did: "I contacted fifteen different counseling centers and they came and did a panel for the ELCA pastors in two counties. The counselors introduced themselves and told about their counseling center." Pastor Amy found that most mental health professionals were open to be on the panel. Another study participant encouraged churches to "get together and sign a contract with a telemedicine company" to increase access to services.[34]

Jeff (see final chapter) details how his church connected to resources. On the launch day of be nice.Faith, the church set up fifteen to twenty tables in the main sanctuary staffed by personnel from local counseling services, hospitals, and Young Life. The church also had "safe pods" so that people with questions for themselves or loved ones could meet privately with one of six local counselors who donated their time to the church on that Sunday.

The last step is to refer to community resources. Pastor Jim Liske encourages collaboration. He says,

> We need to collaborate. We need to understand all the good people in our community. . . . . Every person sitting in the pew needs to have a few business cards, needs to have the ability to say, "Here is someone who you can call."

One of the most important resources everyone in church needs to know about is the 988 Suicide & Crisis Lifeline (https://988lifeline.org/). Anyone can call, anyone. Callers are connected to one of 200 accredited crisis centers.[35] There is a lot of research evidence that crisis lines help prevent suicide.[36]

---

34. Unpublished interview from Mason et al., "How Counselors Can Help."

35. See https://988lifeline.org/our-network/; Draper, *National Best Practices*.

36. Gould et al., "Suicidal Crisis Callers"; Kalafat et al., "Evaluation of Crisis Hotline Outcomes"; Ramchand et al., "Characteristics and Proximal Outcomes of Calls"; Gould et al., "Helping Callers."

But only about 50 percent of callers to the lifeline utilize follow-up mental health care.[37] Churches can monitor follow-up because referrals also communicate hope to congregants who may have lost hope. One pastor said, "If it does seem reasonable that life could be better, then it seems to me part of my job is helping the person get the supportive resources they need and helping them imagine an alternate and better future."[38] This is an important step in helping shift a suicidal person to a hopeful narrative. Pastors try to shift suicidal congregants "towards hope, recovery, or redemptive suffering. . . . [A congregant] needs help understanding that she has options."[39]

In this chapter we put in place the rest of the frame for suicide intervention: connection to community resources. In the next chapter, we'll begin to build in the safety features of the building by ministering to suicide loss survivors.

Discussion Questions

1. Have you ever been referred to a specialist? How did that go? What makes referrals hard to navigate? What makes referrals easier to navigate?

2. Have you ever been referred to a specialist and did not follow through? Why?

3. What are the cultural beliefs in your community about mental health and suicide? How would those beliefs play into referrals?

4. What would help you feel comfortable enough to call the 988 Suicide & Crisis Lifeline?

Take Stock of Your Church

1. What is your church's theological attitude about mental health and suicide? How would that attitude play into referrals? How would you argue theologically to your church leadership that becoming a well-networked church is vital?

37. Gould et al., "National Suicide Prevention Lifeline."
38. Mason et al., "Moral Deliberations," 339.
39. Mason et al., "Moral Deliberations," 340.

2. What knowledge about mental health and suicide does your church have? What knowledge does it need to have?

3. What cultural beliefs in your community must you be aware of and be sensitive to? How would you contextualize your networks in your community?

4. How would you foster relationships between your church and community resources?

5. How would you develop and then keep a list of community resources up to date?

Resources

Clinical Pastoral Education. https://acpe.edu/

The National Action Alliance Faith Communities Task Force has information and resources which can be accessed here: https://theactionalliance.org/task-force/faith-communities.

988 Suicide & Crisis Lifeline. https://988lifeline.org/

Mental Health Ministry

While this book is focused on suicide prevention, many churches engage suicide prevention through a mental health ministry. If you'd like to learn more about how churches can be a resource for people with a mental health condition, and how to respond with compassion and care, here are some resources. These resources sometimes include suicide prevention resources.

Gregg-Schroeder, Susan. *Mental Illness and Families of Faith: How Congregations Can Respond (Resource/Study Guide for Clergy and Communities of Faith)*: http://www.mentalhealthministries.net/resources/study_guide/mental_illness_study_guide.pdf.

The Interfaith Network on Mental Illness. http://inmi.us/

Mental Health First Aid. https://www.mentalhealthfirstaid.org/

NAMI Faith Net is an interfaith resource for all faith traditions who wish to encourage faith communities to be welcoming and supportive of person and families living with mental illness. https://www.nami.org/Get-Involved/NAMI-FaithNet

Matthew Stanford, PhD, offers a free program for churches called Gateway to Hope. https://mentalhealthgateway.org/gateway-to-hope/

United Church of Christ Mental Health Network. https://www.mhn-ucc.org/

Part 3: **Postvention**

CHAPTER 7

Essential Element 6: A Ministering Church

> Do not judge, or you too will be judged. For in the same way you
> judge others, you will be judged, and with the measure you use, it
> will be measured to you. (Matt 7:1–2)

Dr. Melinda Moore is a psychologist and professor who lost her husband to suicide in 1996. She calls that time "the Dark Ages of Suicide Prevention" when a national toll-free number did not even exist. Melinda was newly married and working in public health in May 1996 when the Navy's top admiral, Jeremy Michael Boorda, killed himself in the Washington Navy Yard. She says, "I remember not understanding why somebody would kill themselves." She says she had her own stigmas and myths about suicide following her brother's best friend's suicide when she was growing up, and another very close family friend's suicide when Melinda was in college. Thirteen days after Admiral Boorda's death, her husband killed himself very unexpectedly. Melinda describes the loss of her husband to suicide as traumatic. She desperately wanted to process suicide within the context of her faith. She says,

> After my personal introduction to suicide, I was looking for resources in my community on how to understand suicide. But no one around me, my therapist, my doctor, could help me understand suicide. I remember going to Mass and kneeling at the altar and marrying my suffering with Christ on the cross. That was the only place I felt peace.

She reached out to people, but encountered silence. She says,

> Nobody at work would talk to me about it. It was like I was a pariah. Suicide was catching or whatever taint I had acquired as a result of this experience changed my life profoundly. It was so isolating on top of this incredible trauma. . . . People of faith at

> work would see me walking down the hallway, and turn and walk
> in the opposite direction. People were very uncomfortable around
> me. It was clear to me that everyone was uncomfortable. There was
> huge ignorance and huge fear. I saw it consistently at work, [in]
> my medical providers, my church family. People didn't talk to me.

Despite the silence at her church, she found comfort in her faith. She asked her priest, "Wouldn't it be great if we had a support group for people with tremendous losses?" The priest dismissed the idea "as if I had said something that was wrong." But Melinda was not easily discouraged. "I realized that those of us going through difficult circumstances really need to understand suicide in the context of our faith." While she was convinced of the loving nature of God, she continued to ask a number of priests, "Why would God do this to Conor? Why would God do this to me? I don't know how to think about suicide within the context of my faith."

She remembers gratefully that she received compassion from a few people. She is deeply grateful to Father Stephen Hays, who performed a Month's Mind Mass one month after Conor's death. At the beginning of the Mass, Father Stephen Hays said, "Conor is with God by virtue of his baptism." These words helped set the stage for her healing. Another healing moment was in talking to Father Bill Maroon from whom she first experienced true compassion. She says,

> All he did was show compassion. He cried with me. We talked
> about Job. He didn't preach. Finally, I accepted the mystery. That
> was the beginning of healing and understanding that there is a
> great deal of diversity of experience and understanding of suicide
> within the Church. My therapist couldn't help me, my doctor
> couldn't, my family couldn't, my friends couldn't. The isolation
> and invalidation were overwhelming.

Following this experience, she focused on healing for two years. "I knew I had to heal." During these two years, as a loss survivor, she continued to notice people not talking to her. She felt alone and rejected. She says that loss survivors interpret the silence as "your concerns are not valid. You shouldn't be grieving. There is something wrong with you."

She struggles to understand what holds clergy back from showing compassion to loss survivors. "Given the high stakes of spiritual situations, I don't know why there is no recognition that there has to be an approach or an accepted theology to help priests in these moments." As she healed, she looked for resources which were far and few between.

"What struck me was the lack of information about surviving suicide." Melinda found a very helpful book *Suicide, Survivors: A Guide for Those Left Behind*, by Adina Wrobleski. The book captured Melinda's experience as a loss survivor and helped her deal with misplaced guilt over Conor's death. The book was important because long-term care from clergy was absent. "The care was so inconsistent." She now gets ongoing support from fellow suicide prevention advocates. "My long-term pastoral care is with people I am colleagues with."

Melinda has been the co-lead of the National Action Alliance for Suicide Prevention Faith Communities Task Force. She is an advocate for the church to be involved in suicide prevention. She says, "It's important to be part of the change within." She adds,

> As a Catholic, I get pro-life messages all the time. I wish there was some understanding of suicide being a pro-life issue. If you are pro-life, you are already a suicide prevention advocate. I wish the Catholic Church would be consistent in their pro-life stance. I wish the Pope would say something. I wish the Church understood as compassionate human beings the complex problems of suicide and suicide bereavement.

She laments the message from the Church to people who are suffering. The message these people get are based in stigma:

> Because you are struggling, you are unworthy. You do not belong to any community, your faith community, your family, your friends, and as a result you are a burden on us and everybody around us. Your existence is a burden.

Melinda calls on the Church to communicate a different message and show compassion to suffering people.[1]

Because ministering to survivors is such an important aspect of church ministry, and because grieving is different for each person, let's hear from another loss survivor.

Rev. Dr. Ken Myers and his wife are both pastors. He first heard about his daughter's suicide while driving home on a Thursday afternoon. The news spread quickly within his and his wife's churches. He said, "Once you tell one person, it spreads like wildfire." Besides absorbing this

---

1. Author interview with Dr. Melinda Moore, March 2, 2021. Moore (PhD, Catholic University of America) is an associate professor of Psychology at Eastern Kentucky University, a licensed psychologist, and has been the co-lead for the National Action Alliance for Suicide Prevention Faith Communities Task Force.

tragic news, Pastor Ken was confronted by several challenges, like people wanting to come to his house, or his wife and he having different ways of grieving. His wife grieves in private. Apart from family and close friends, she doesn't like people "all up on her." Despite this, they felt the support of the church. "We got a lot, a lot, a lot of food, and flowers, and texts and calls. We sensed everyone's prayers. We felt people's love." Pastor Ken felt the support of the district superintendent when she released him from preaching the following Sunday. He felt very supported by the many folks who expressed their love to him and his wife.

When friends and family members came to the house, no one talked about how his daughter died. As Pastor Ken reflects back, he says, "It might not have been appropriate at the time. I don't know how it would have been helpful to talk about the suicide." He talked with a very close friend about his misdirected sense of responsibility for the death.

Both Pastor Ken and his wife have changed churches, located in new towns. Pastor Ken understands that his wife wanted to get away from the area where they and their daughter had lived, because living there "keeps drudging things up." They moved to new churches where people don't know about the suicide. Pastor Ken hasn't experienced long-term care because people don't know of their loss.

But Pastor Ken has noticed that God brings reminders of the suicide to bring more healing. Pastor Ken and his wife were at a conference where the speaker talked about his son's death by Russian roulette. Pastor Ken felt that God was peeling back "another layer of the onion" by providing a safe place to grieve. He describes the healing moments:

> I'm trying to do my best to hold back my tears, and I couldn't anymore. It was a powerfully healing moment. The tears were healing. We felt love and support because friends who knew their story immediately began praying for them.

Their friends didn't know what else to do besides pray and "to let God do what God does." Pastor Ken adds,

> I don't know if there was anything anyone could do in that moment. What was so completely healing in that moment was I was in a safe place where I could just cry. The speaker's willingness to share that incredibly painful moment was healing. I'm wondering if that wasn't a witness to me and my wife that it's okay to share those painful things because, in the process of doing that, people can identify with you in the sense that we've had our

painful experiences, not necessarily the same thing, we too had our painful experiences that have been somewhat shameful, and the release in telling that story is incredibly healing and powerful.

Pastor Ken believes that people don't share their stories about suicide because of shame attached to suicide. He says,

> Some folks just don't talk about it. And I think it might be because of the powerful emotions that come with it, and the fear that expressing those emotions, whether it's anger or deep sorrow and grief and whatever it might be that they're experiencing, they don't want that to come out. They are doing everything they can do to push that down. Pushing the emotions down is fueled by shame, the deep sense of shame that they are experiencing, that if we don't talk about this, then it doesn't exist.

Pastor Ken reflects on another suicide when he was a young pastor. At that time, he was "green as the grass in ministry." One of his congregants lost her twenty-four-year-old son to suicide. The police called Pastor Ken. He could hear the mother "screaming in the background." He remembers driving to the congregant's home saying to himself, "I have no idea what to say or do to help these grieving folks." He reflects back and realizes he had a deep sense of peace that he was not to say anything. "I was convinced that nothing I would say would bring any peace or comfort to that family. It was all about the ministry of presence." When people are afraid of what to say, or that they'll say something stupid, he advises them,

> You don't have to say anything. All you have to do is just go and be with the people who are grieving. Just let them know that you are praying for them and that you are supporting them and that you are there for them. I heard God say to me: "Just shut your mouth and be present."

Pastor Ken remembers answering the mother when she asked him: "Do you think my son is in Hell?" He said no because he realized, "There is no theological explanation that is needed here. She is not at a place where she could receive it if she wanted to." Pastor Ken officiated at the funeral where he "brought God's love and peace and offered no explanation." He said, "There is no way any of us can know or understand why her son did this. But we know a God who is faithful in the midst of it." He remembered the teaching he got from his own pastor growing up who said, "Funerals are for the living, not for the dead."[2]

In this chapter, we'll start installing the safety features in a suicide-safe church, safety features like smoke detectors that prevent tragedy. This is our first postvention step: ministering to those who have lost a loved one to suicide and to the community as a whole. Postvention is everything a church does when caring for a person and community following a suicide. Postvention requires pastors to learn how to conduct funeral or memorial services, and requires everyone in the church to learn how to minister to those who have lost a loved one to suicide.

Why Do Churches Need to Minister to Loss Survivors?

A person who loses a loved one to suicide, whether family or friend, is a "loss survivor," short for "survivor of suicide loss." Why do churches need to know about how to minister to loss survivors?

As we saw in the Introduction, suicide happens in churches. Matthew Warren took his life. Pastors have died by suicide.[3] Pastors have told us about the suicide deaths they have experienced in churches and suicide funerals they have officiated.[4] If a suicide death happens in a church, every congregant is a loss survivor.

In any group (including a church), 4 percent (4.3 percent) of group members will be loss survivors in one year, and 22 percent (21.8 percent) will be loss survivors in their lifetime.[5] Most lose friends or peers; a few lose family members. Those numbers add up to a lot of people who have lost someone to suicide. Dr. Melinda Moore says each suicide results in 135 loss survivors.[6] And some of those people are in church.

2. Author interview with Rev. Dr. Ken Myers, February 18, 2021. Myers (PhD, University of Florida) is an ordained pastor in the United Methodist Church, a trained counselor, and a counselor educator.

3. Pastor Andrew Stocklein, Pastor Jarrid Wilson, and Pastor Seve Austin died by suicide.

4. Mason et al., "Clergy as Suicide Prevention Gatekeepers"; Mason et al., "Clergy Use of Suicide Prevention Competencies"; Mason et al., "Clergy Referral of Suicidal Individuals"; Mason et al., "Developmental Model"; Gibson and Mason, *Preaching Hope in Darkness.*

5. Andriessen, "Prevalence of Exposure to Suicide."

6. Cerel et al., "How Many People Are Exposed to Suicide?"

Why is this a problem for churches? Losing a loved one to suicide brings on excruciating grief. This kind of grief is called complicated or prolonged grief. What is this type of grief? Complicated[7] or prolonged grief[8] includes regular grief plus intense longing for the deceased, re-occurring thoughts or images about the deceased, intense feelings of anger and guilt, avoidance of situations, people and places that remind of the deceased, difficulty finding meaning in life *and suicidal thinking*. Those closest to the person who died are at risk for depression, anxiety, and *suicidal behavior*. Loss survivors' grief includes intrusive preoccupation with the circumstances of the loss, self-blame, avoidance of previously shared activities, and inadequate adaptation to the loss.[9] Grief is prolonged because bereaved people are not able to adapt to or accept the finality of their loss and the grieving process is complicated, slowed, or halted.[10]

The suicidal thinking in complicated or prolonged grief makes ministering to a loss survivor an essential element in suicide prevention because it can prevent another suicide. The National Strategy for Suicide Prevention emphasizes that support for those bereaved by suicide is an important strategy for suicide prevention.[11] That is why postvention is so important and why a church needs to know how to minister to survivors of suicide loss.

One of the reasons loss survivors' grief is more intense than other grief is that loss survivors experience more feelings of rejection, a greater need to conceal the cause of the death, and more shame, blaming, and social stigmatization than other survivor groups; less social support can complicate adaptation to the loss.[12] A pastor who was interviewed for one of our studies said,

> Death always pulls at the fabric of our relationships, at the fabric of our faith. But, suicide is in a class by itself because, "I should have known," "I should have done something," "What are people going to think?" A lot of "why" questions and additional pain associated

---

7. Young et al., "Suicide Bereavement and Complicated Grief."

8. Andriessen et al., "Effectiveness of Interventions."

9. Linde et al., "Grief Interventions."

10. Linde et al., "Grief Interventions."

11. US Department of Health and Human Services, *2012 National Strategy for Suicide Prevention*.

12. Linde et al., "Grief Interventions."

with that, which just means being a lot more intentional about listening and loving and offering support for as long as it takes.[13]

But why do some churches not support loss survivors? As we saw in chapter 2, stigma and shame may keep loss survivors from reaching out for support.[14] And fellow congregants may not reach out to them. Suicide also creates "social ambiguity" which occurs when "the norms for appropriate behavior in a given social situation are unclear."[15] People generally don't know what to do for loss survivors, and this lack of clarity creates an awkward and uncomfortable feeling for everyone. Loss survivors notice that expressions of support are noticeably absent, lukewarm in tone, or reluctantly supplied and slow in coming from people loss survivors are counting on when the going gets tough.[16] If loss survivors have to ask for support, they may feel resentment and betrayal. Following their daughter's suicide attempt, a Christian family never received any support from their church, though their daughter's unchurched karate teacher brought a meal.[17]

What Is Helpful for Loss Survivors?

Support in Their Grieving

Loss survivors should get what all grieving people need. They should get the opportunity to grieve in their own way.[18] They should get the support to talk about their loved one holistically, not just how they died. They may want to discuss the guilt of "Could I have done something?" They should get tangible help like meals and child care.

They should also get professional help. Only about half of loss survivors get formal help in their grief,[19] perhaps because there is still a lack of research evidence about what is most helpful in suicide bereavement. One type of help are self-help groups with other loss survivors that include supportive, therapeutic, and educational aspects.[20] Self-help groups can

13. Unpublished interview from Mason et al., "How Counselors Can Help."

14. Andriessen et al., "Effectiveness of Interventions"; Juth et al., "Social Constraints."

15. Jordan and Baugher, *After Suicide Loss*, 61–62.

16. Thoits, "Mechanisms Linking Social Ties and Support."

17. Gibson and Mason, *Preaching Hope in Darkness*, 83.

18. Goldman, "Breaking the Silence."

19. Linde et al., "Grief Interventions."

20. Andriessen et al., "Effectiveness of Interventions."

help reduce the intensity of grief.[21] Dr. Melinda leads such a group. Some churches offer loss survivor groups.[22] Another possible type of help is writing about the bereavement experiences four times for fifteen minutes each time over a period of two weeks, guided by a trained facilitator.[23]

Loss survivors may decide to change churches. Leaving church is not a necessity, but it is not unusual. Churches need to be ready that part of their ministry might be to let the loss survivor go to another church. One reason survivors leave a church is to avoid situations, people, and places that remind them of the suicide loss. One pastor gave the example of a husband staying at the church while the wife attended another church. The wife told the pastor, "I see you up in front of the congregation in those robes and I go back to that [memorial] service. I can't help it . . . and it's just too painful."[24] This pastor made sure that this survivor was supported in another church. He said, "I knew that the best way for me to pastor her was not to be her pastor. That I needed to see that she was pastored."[25]

Another reason loss survivors leave a church is unmet expectations. In one self-help group, within two years of a suicide, at least 80 percent of survivors had either left the church they were attending and joined another or stopped attending church altogether. The two most common reasons for leaving were (1) disappointment due to unmet expectations and (2) criticism or judgmental attitudes and treatment.[26] One survivor couple did not receive their pastor's care and ended up leaving the church because "the support wasn't there anymore."[27] Another survivor pointed out, "You get the opportunity to find out who your true friends are. And some people are not your true friends."

We have found that loss survivors often change churches because they "aren't the same people anymore" following a suicide.[28] A suicide loss changes people. Because they are changed, loss survivors may not want to remain friends with people who couldn't grieve with them because "it's

21. Linde et al., "Grief Interventions."

22. Unpublished interview from Mason et al., "How Counselors Can Help."

23. Pennebaker and Beall, "Confronting a Traumatic Event."

24. Gibson and Mason, *Preaching Hope in Darkness*, 89.

25. Gibson and Mason, *Preaching Hope in Darkness*, 89.

26. Biebel and Foster, *Finding Your Way*, 169.

27. Gibson and Mason, *Preaching Hope in Darkness*, 89.

28. Gibson and Mason, *Preaching Hope in Darkness*, 89.

burdensome for [the friends]."[29] And as survivors change, they may seek out a new set of friends.

Some loss survivors might not leave the church but may be reluctant to return to church. It's important to call and invite survivors back to church when they are ready. One survivor advised, "Don't stop trying . . . Keep inviting them. Don't lose sight of them."[30]

Pastor Ken says that talking about suicide and giving loss survivors the freedom to talk about suicide is important. But it's not just suicide. Pastor Ken says, "It's death in general. People don't like to talk to other people about death. The number one fear is I don't know what to say." In that case, Pastor Ken advises saying nothing and offering a ministry of presence,

> You don't have to say anything. All you have to do is just go and be with the people who are grieving. Just let them know that you are praying for them and that you are supporting them and that you are there for them.

A "ministry of presence" is just being present or just listening. Listening provides a safe place for the loss survivor to grieve. In this ministry of presence, it is fine to mention positive memories of the person who died by suicide. The person who died was so much more than the way they died. But take your cues from the grieving loss survivor. Because grief is unique, find out what would be helpful for the loss survivor.

In *Preventing Suicide*,[31] I advise that it's best to avoid Christian platitudes like "God doesn't give you more than you can handle," or, "God wanted your loved one in heaven." Platitudes do not acknowledge suffering. "Like vinegar on a wound is one who sings songs to a heavy heart" (Prov 25:20). It's best instead to say simply, "I'm so sorry for your loss."

The Suicide Funeral

One of the difficult parts of a suicide death is the funeral. Rabbi Dan Roberts challenges faith leaders to see the funeral as an important moment in the life of a family and the life of the church. He writes,

> A suicide funeral may be one of the most meaningful moments in your career and one in which you can have great impact. You

29. Gibson and Mason, *Preaching Hope in Darkness*, 89.

30. Gibson and Mason, *Preaching Hope in Darkness*, 89.

31. Mason, *Preventing Suicide*, ch. 9.

will not only be a comfort to family and friends, you can help them come to terms with what appears to be a senseless moment. Moreover, you have the potential to prevent contagion. Your words can prevent another human being from contemplating suicide as a solution to their darkened world. It is a powerful moment in your career, in your life.[32]

In the funeral it is appropriate to encourage funeral attendees to look around to find someone they can reach out to for help. Challenge the belief that each person should be self-sufficient. A study participant advises to balance the need to mention suicide in the funeral while recognizing that "a person is not defined by a single act in their life."[33]

Telling Children

One of the questions that is often raised is how much to tell children. Experts advise that you tell the child about the suicide death, and that children not hear about the suicide from someone else. This is what Donna L. Schuurman advised.[34] Donna is the executive director emeritus of the Dougy Center, which provides grief support to children, teens, young adults, and their families.

> I can share what children at the Dougy Center in our "Healing after a suicide death" group have consistently told us since we first started the group in 1986: "Tell us the truth. Don't lie to us. Answer our questions honestly."
>
> To date, in the thirty-four years I've been associated with the Dougy Center, and from my days in the suicide bereavement group, I have not heard one child ever say, "I'm glad they didn't tell me the truth," or, "It was good that they lied to me," but I have heard many say that it was hard enough to experience the death of their parent or sibling, and then the added piece about being lied to, or having truth withheld, complicated things for them. Additionally, they consistently express that they find themselves wondering what else their parent/adult caregiver is either withholding or lying to them about.

32. Roberts, "Preparing a Eulogy or Memorial Service," 13.

33. Unpublished interview from Mason et al., "How Counselors Can Help."

34. Email to the Suicidology listserv on Friday, February 7, 2020. Used with permission.

I will add that while we should answer their questions honestly, we don't need to give any information they haven't asked about since they may not be ready to hear it. If we create the atmosphere where we say and demonstrate that we will answer anything they ask, they will ask when they're ready.

An additional piece to consider is that with social media, it is more likely than not that children will hear about the means of their parent's death from another child or someone else, or (hopefully not) on social media. It is near impossible to keep "secrets" like this in the age of social media, so the question becomes who would you like your child to hear the truth from? Another child in their class, Snapchat, or . . . you?

I would say something like this to a parent: *I can understand your concern about sharing that your (husband/partner/wife/ spouse) died of suicide . . . no one would ever want to have to tell their child that their (father/mother/foster parent, etc.) has died, and it can be hard to understand and explain suicide to a child. So I am not suggesting this is an easy thing to do. What I can share is that it is extremely likely that your child will hear information about this from someone else ~ someone in their school, another kid who overheard an adult talking about it, or perhaps even through social media. It's extremely hard to keep information private with the advent of all the social media outlets. If your child hears from someone else, he/she/they may be upset or angry with you that others knew and you didn't tell them him/her/them. They may well wonder what else you're keeping from them, and it can lead to trust issues . . . at the same time, I would advise you to share gently, and in pieces, as they ask questions, rather than overwhelming them with information they may not be ready to hear or able to process. So, start with saying that you have some really hard, sad news; that your father/ mother/other has died . . . if/when they ask "how?" you can say they died of suicide . . . or you could say "he shot himself" or "she jumped off a bridge" or "they took too many pills and died," depending on the age/experience/maturity level of the child.*

How to explain suicide to a child? It's not easy, and will depend on their developmental (and perhaps to some degree, chronological) age, as well as other factors, including whether or not the person who died had been displaying actions that the child observed or was part of, for example over-using substances around the child, being arrested in front of the child, etc. In that case I might say " . . . as you know, Daddy was having a really hard time not drinking, and when he was drinking he wasn't always as nice as he was when he wasn't drinking . . . " If there are no prior signs, or if the child was not privy to any prior signs that their parent might be feeling suicidal, I would say something like "Daddy was struggling with a lot of things in his life that caused him a lot of pain. The pain he was in kind of took over; he couldn't see or imagine that anything would help him not be in pain, and he shot himself."

I hope this is helpful.

With care,
Donna

A Couple Last Thoughts

Some loss survivors want to talk about their story of loss and some don't. One of our study participants said,

> I think those of us who are suicide loss survivors, we either want to be really engaged in that field and share our own story or we don't want to talk about it anymore. And in my world where my passion comes from is, I don't want to tell my story. I want to share an action plan that can actually save somebody's life.[35]

Pastor Amy adds that the church can minister to loss survivors beyond the church. She says,

> It is important for churches to offer care and support to those who are caring for those impacted by suicide. For example, when there is a suicide in a school, find a way, maybe an email or leave a voice mail for the school staff, just saying that you are thinking about them and praying for them as they are caring for students, teachers and staff. Or if a pastor leads a funeral, reach out and just say those simple things, that you are offering prayers for them. The same can be done for funeral directors. Or for anyone involved in law enforcement or first responders. After a death in a community, offering a prayer in worship for the first responders who come to homes and help when there is a death, offering a word of thanks to people [who are caring for those impacted by suicide].

In this chapter, we started installing postvention safety devices, namely ministering to suicide loss survivors. In the next chapter, we'll install one

---

35. Unpublished interview from Mason et al., "How Counselors Can Help."

more safety device: being alert to the risks of suicide contagion. We'll also discuss how to manage guilt and commit to Sabbath rest.

Discussion Questions

1. Have you ever grieved? What is your style of grieving?

2. Have you ever experienced "social ambiguity," where you didn't know what to do in the situation? What did you do?

3. Have you ever been on the receiving end of ministry of presence? Have you ever ministered with your presence? How did that go?

4. What are some platitudes that you have heard? (e.g., "She is in the Lord's hands"; "God will work it out for your good"; "I know how you feel"; "Get over it and get on with your life"; "Take your troubles to God.")

Take Stock of Your Church

1. How would your church handle a loss survivor leaving your church?

2. How would your church counteract the stigma and shame that a loss survivor might experience?

3. Rate your church's capacity to listen and be present.

4. Rate your church's capacity to provide practical helps to loss survivors.

5. Rate your church's capacity to plan a funeral following a suicide that helps listeners learn to reach out for help.

6. Rate your church's capacity to tell the truth to children.

Resources

988 Suicide & Crisis Lifeline. https://988lifeline.org/

Grief Support Groups

The Compassionate Friends. https://www.compassionatefriends.org/
Dougy center. https://www.dougy.org/about/our-story/mission-history

Survivor support groups at

American Association of Suicidology. https://suicidology.org/resources/support-groups/
American Foundation of Suicide Prevention. https://afsp.org/find-a-support-group/

Suicide Funeral Resources

Gibson, Scott, and Karen Mason. *Preaching Hope in Darkness: Help for Pastors in Addressing Suicide from the Pulpit*. Bellingham: Lexham, 2020.
Moore, Melinda, and Daniel A. Roberts, eds. *The Suicide Funeral (Or Memorial Service): Honoring Their Memory, Comforting Their Survivors*. Eugene, OR: Resource, 2017.
Suicide Prevention Resource Center. *After a Suicide: Recommendations for Religious Services and Other Public Memorial Observances*. Newton, MA: Education Development Center, Inc., 2004.

Books

Jordan, Jack, and Bob Baugher. *After Suicide Loss: Coping with your Grief*. Newcastle: Caring People, 2016.
Sands, Diana. *Red Chocolate Elephants: For Children Bereaved by Suicide*. Belmont: Karridale Pty Limited, 2010.
Spexarth, Kristen. *Passing Reflection*, Vol. 3: *Surviving Suicide Loss Through Mindfulness*. New York: Big Think Media, 2016.

Essential Element 7: A Monitoring Church

> Those parts of the body that seem to be weaker are indispensable, and the parts that we think are less honorable we treat with special honor. And the parts that are unpresentable are treated with special modesty, while our presentable parts need no special treatment. But God has put the body together, giving greater honor to the parts that lacked it, so that there should be no division in the body, but that its parts should have equal concern for each other. If one part suffers, every part suffers with it; if one part is honored, every part rejoices with it. (1 Cor 12:22–26)

Former Pastor Fe Anam Avis tells his story in the book *A Second Day*. He became involved in suicide prevention when, over the Thanksgiving holiday, a young man in the local high school killed himself. Then, over Christmas there was a second suicide, and then in June a third one. During a seven-month period, three students from a high school of three hundred killed themselves. He was the senior pastor of the only church located in the community.

After the third suicide, Fe and his psychologist friend said, "Somebody needs to do something about this." They wondered, "Who is responsible for the overall well-being of the community?" They realized the answer is complicated because the many dimensions of suicide mean no one community group is tasked to do something about it. Fe says,

> Suicide has a mental health dimension. It has a political side to it, but political leaders don't want to own up to it happening in their community. There is an economic side to it because people won't want to move into the community because suicide happens there. There is a medical side to it, there are the parents, there is a spiritual side to it.

Fe goes on to say,

> Everyone was in their compartments. So my friend and I put together a Community Response Team, a multi-disciplinary professional group that would get together. We published educational articles in the local newspaper. We started meeting with the school superintendent. We had conversations with mental health folks. We began to put together a strategy.

Fe networked with others in his region. Then the community-based efforts expanded to their state. He says, "Connecting to others is key." He also was trained in LivingWorks ASIST and began training others, including clergy. His trainings of clergy expanded into Soul Shop, a faith-based suicide prevention training for churches.[1]

Some people wonder if copycat suicides really happen. There is extensive evidence for copycat suicide attempts or deaths. The first step in preventing these is to be aware when exposure happens, and the second step is to know who is most vulnerable to copying suicidal behavior, who should be monitored. In this chapter we'll install the last essential safety device in a suicide-safe church: being alert to the risks of copycat suicide. We'll also discuss how to manage guilt and observe the Sabbath in the context of suicide. Managing copycat behavior, guilt, and Sabbath are essential elements in preventing further suicidal behavior.

Why Is Copycat Suicide a Problem?

Clergy tell us that they are involved in an average of two[2] to three suicide deaths across their professional experience, with 62 percent experiencing at least one suicide death.[3] Most say they have not experienced a copycat suicide.[4] However, as Fe tells his story, it obviously can be part of a pastor's and church's experience.

---

1. Author interview with Fe Anam Avis, February 16, 2021. Fe Anam Avis is retired. He has been a Presbyterian pastor, a suicide prevention trainer and activist, and a consultant to churches. He is an author of five books and the founder of Soul Shop.

2. Mason et al., "Clergy Use of Suicide Prevention Competencies."

3. Mason et al., "Clergy as Suicide Prevention Gatekeepers."

4. Mason et al., "Clergy as Suicide Prevention Gatekeepers."

What Do We Know about Copycat Suicide in the US?

What is a copycat suicide attempt or death? It is one that occurs closely in time and place to another. How many suicide attempts or deaths need to happen in order to qualify as copycat? That number is not hard and fast. A copycat or cluster is "a group of suicides or suicide attempts, or both, that occur closer together in time and space than would normally be expected in a given community."[5] The number is not what is important. What is important is that one suicide attempt or death may influence another.

It is important for churches to understand two aspects of copycat suicidal behavior: exposure and vulnerability.

Exposure

A copycat suicide attempt or death can only happen when a vulnerable person is exposed to a suicide attempt or death. The exposure can happen through the media, through a peer group, or through family.[6] For example, after Robin Williams took his life, a 9.85 percent increase in suicides was observed among males and people aged thirty to forty-four years old.[7] After Netflix released *13 Reasons Why*, which depicts a high school student's suicide, there was a 28.9 percent increase in suicide rates among US youth ages ten to seventeen in the month (April 2017) after its release, even after accounting for ongoing trends in suicide rates.[8] Studies have also shown an increase in suicide risk following the suicide of a peer,[9] a sibling,[10] or other family members.[11]

5. Centers for Disease Control and Prevention, "CDC Recommendations for a Community Plan."

6. Mościcki, "Epidemiology of Suicide"; Stack, "Media Coverage"; Stack, "Suicide in the Media."

7. Fink et al., "Increase in Suicides."

8. Bridge et al., "Association between the Release of Netflix's *13 Reasons Why*."

9. Abrutyn and Mueller, "Are Suicidal Behaviors Contagious in Adolescence?"

10. Rostila et al., "Suicide Following the Death of a Sibling."

11. Qin, "Relationship of Suicide Risk to Family History"; Niederkrotenthaler et al., "Exposure to Parental Mortality."

Vulnerability

But not everyone exposed to it copies suicidal behavior. Most people who heard about Robin Williams' suicide on the news did not copy it. Why not? Because not everyone is equally vulnerable to that exposure. Contagion and transmission happen to the vulnerable. But who are the vulnerable? During the pandemic, we have learned that people with lower immune systems because of age or an underlying health condition are at increased risk of a severe case of COVID-19.[12] Who is more vulnerable to suicide contagion?

Young People

Vulnerable individuals can include anyone, but the most vulnerable group is young people. Most suicide clusters happen in adolescents and young adults.[13] Girls seem to be more vulnerable to suicide suggestion than boys.[14] On average, adolescent girls are 2.13 times more likely to report suicidal *thoughts* after experiencing a family member's attempted suicide and 1.56 times more likely to report suicidal *thoughts* after experiencing a friend's suicide attempt. Girls' suicide *attempts*, on average, are significantly related to friends' suicide attempts, though not family members' attempts.[15] For boys, experiencing a friend's suicide attempt renders boys 1.65 times more likely to report suicidal *thoughts*; the suicide attempt of a family-based role model has no effect.[16] Friends appear to be more powerful role models for both boys and girls. Researchers think that exposure to suicidal behavior might teach young people new ways to deal with emotional distress; namely, by becoming suicidal.[17] One study participant cautions ministers about how they talk about suicide. He said,

> You can inadvertently glorify [suicide] in the eye of someone dealing with depression. If you are not careful, you can almost encourage a teenager in the way their mind is processing stuff. They can twist it to think it is an acceptable solution. So you have to talk

12. See "COVID-19 Information for Specific Groups of People."
13. Mościcki, "Epidemiology of Suicide," 49.
14. Abrutyn and Mueller, "Are Suicidal Behaviors Contagious in Adolescence?"
15. Abrutyn and Mueller, "Are Suicidal Behaviors Contagious in Adolescence?"
16. Abrutyn and Mueller, "Are Suicidal Behaviors Contagious in Adolescence?"
17. Abrutyn and Mueller, "Are Suicidal Behaviors Contagious in Adolescence?"

about it in a way that really connects with the person, and you have to be careful how you talk about it.[18]

But why young people? It might be that young people are particularly sensitive to the way suicide is portrayed in popular media.[19] It might also be that young people are seeking to be "somebody." A young woman's suicide in 1839 at the Monument to the Great Fire of London was followed by a boy's suicide attempt. He explained later, "I wished to be talked of, like the woman who killed herself at the monument!"[20]

The vulnerability after exposure does not last long term. For boys and girls, the impact of the suicide attempt of a role model, whether a family member or friend, lasts at least one year, though this might last longer for girls.[21] Six years later, there is little evidence that experiencing the suicide attempt of a role model has an effect over the long run, except perhaps for girls who are in emotional distress.[22]

Who Else Is Vulnerable?

Fe points out that others might also be vulnerable. Anyone who has lost someone to suicide or has been suicidal themselves can be at risk. He says,

> If you have a suicide in your congregation, . . . you've got people at higher risk. . . . That suicide has triggered people who have lost someone in the past, or have been suicidal in the past, so you've got some healing work to do.

A church has to think about who in their congregation is vulnerable. Vulnerable congregants could be people already touched by suicide, but also who resemble the person who died by suicide in some way. For example, a male with a degenerative disease and depression might be a vulnerable congregant following Robin Williams' suicide. A church needs to think broadly about who might be vulnerable.

18. Unpublished interview from Mason et al., "How Counselors Can Help."

19. Lisa Horowitz, PhD, quoted in "Release of '13 Reasons Why' Associated with Increase in Youth Suicide Rates."

20. Nicoletti, "Morbid Topographies," 13–14.

21. Abrutyn and Mueller, "Are Suicidal Behaviors Contagious in Adolescence?"

22. Abrutyn and Mueller, "Are Suicidal Behaviors Contagious in Adolescence?"

How Do We Prevent Copycat Suicide in a Church?

So what could a church do to manage contagion? It's important to monitor young people and anyone else who might be vulnerable, to carefully manage messaging about suicide, and to get involved at the community level to make sure the whole community coordinates its response.

Monitoring

Following a suicide, churches will likely focus resources to adolescents and young adults.[23] They should monitor how young people are responding to the suicidal behavior, attempt, or death. How do you monitor? Monitoring means looking for signs of suicidal thinking. (Go back to chapter 5 to find out how to become equipped to do this.) Once the church is equipped and skilled to monitor suicidal thinking, it is important to plan time with vulnerable congregants to educate them on the signs of suicide. Be clear about how to reach out, if needed, at home or church or school. Church leadership could send a letter to parents encouraging them to monitor their child. The letter should include the 988 Suicide & Crisis Lifeline number. Go to *Preaching Hope in Darkness*, Appendix I, for an example of how parents can support their student following a suicide.[24] The same can be done for vulnerable adults. Call them to check on them. Organize a forum on suicide prevention for adult congregants.

Some churches prepare for their response to a suicide in advance. "The wisdom of the prudent is to give thought to their steps" (Prov 14:15). Go to *Preaching Hope in Darkness*, Appendix D,[25] to find an example of a church's response protocol for planning how to respond to a suicide.

Messaging

Suicide prevention consultant Fe suggests that preventing contagion has to do with "messaging." He adds,

> [Contagion] has to do with how you balance the celebration of a
> life with pointing out that this is not an appropriate way to end

---

23. Velting and Gould, "Suicide Contagion."

24. Gibson and Mason, *Preaching Hope in Darkness*, 231–34.

25. Gibson and Mason, *Preaching Hope in Darkness*, 167–70.

> your life. How do you do that? In a service, for example, that you
> not only celebrate that life, but let folks in the congregation know
> that if they are considering suicide, they need to get help.

But as Fe points out, "With the second suicide [students] were gathering around the flag pole in the morning and holding hands. They weren't getting much guidance in terms of what to do." Messaging happens not only in funerals, but throughout the grieving process. Reporting on suicide[26] is a resource that every church needs to study at times like these. While these guidelines are focused on media reporting, these guidelines apply to how a church talks about suicide. It is important to avoid detailed descriptions of the suicide, to avoid emphasizing that the deceased is now at peace, to avoid memorializing the deceased in a way that vulnerable people might see suicide as a way to garner recognition in death.[27] Instead, say, "It's sad that the person wasn't able to reach out for help. No problem is so great that it's not possible to work toward a solution." Ask vulnerable congregants to look around and identify who they can reach out to. Say, "We wished that [the person who died] had lived in a society that understood those who suffer from mental or behavioral health problems and supported those who sought help for those problems without stigma or prejudice."[28]

Coordinating with the Community

Suicide prevention consultant Fe suggests that organizing a community response is key. He explains,

> When we had the three suicides in the community, there was no
> real plan in the school for how to deal with the suicides. The first
> one was shoved under the rug. With the second suicide, kids . . .
> weren't getting much guidance in terms of what to do. So we have
> to work in the community to educate folks in these various sub-
> communities for how to respond. It's important that they not . . .
> lionize the life of the person who died, [suggesting] this is an ap-
> propriate way to die. You have to get them guidelines. You can't
> build memorials and the media can't cover the memorials. The
> media needs guidance to know the guidelines. Giving the media
> guidance is important. Also, looking for underlying issues in the

26. See website: https://reportingonsuicide.org/.

27. Suicide Prevention Resource Center, *After a Suicide.*

28. Suicide Prevention Resource Center, *After a Suicide.*

> community when you're able. We had had a hazing in the commu-
> nity. You have to begin to look at the underlying issues and that re-
> quires a longer-term response. The response must be coordinated.

He suggests the community asks itself, "How do we build a community that optimizes life for people?" Churches are key to helping answer questions about how to build an abundant life, a life worth living. Being a part of your community's response to suicide is important, because, as we saw in the Introduction, churches provide the answer to the question: "Why should a person stay alive?" Churches provide a focus on hope in the midst of suffering.

Community involvement comes in a lot of shapes and sizes. Rev. Dr. Sherry Molock works with the National Action Alliance for Suicide Prevention Faith Communities Task Force, as well as the Congressional Black Caucus Task Force on suicide prevention.[29] Find a community group working on suicide prevention and join it. You can go to the Suicide Prevention Resource Center to find what your state is doing,[30] and then join one of your state's efforts.

Guilt and Sabbath

Guilt

Following a suicide, pastors deal with guilt.[31] Early in their careers, pastors might believe, "I should have known and been able to predict or prevent the suicide." Over time, pastors begin to realize that they do not bear that responsibility. Congregants deal with guilt, too.[32] It is important to reflect on the Catholic Church's perspective that a person who dies by suicide may have diminished moral responsibility because of "grave psychological disturbances."[33] If the person who died by suicide has diminished responsibility, then others do not bear guilt.

There are other reasons that you or your church does not bear guilt for a suicide. One is that not all suicidal people reach out for help. Dr. Eli Robins studied 134 suicides deaths during a one-year period (1956–1957)

---

29. Unpublished interview from Mason et al., "How Counselors Can Help."

30. Visit: https://www.sprc.org/states.

31. Mason et al., "Developmental Model."

32. Mason, *Preventing Suicide*, ch. 9.

33. *Catechism of the Catholic Church*, paras. 2282–83.

in the city of St. Louis and in St. Louis County.[34] He found that 69 percent (ninety-three people) communicated their intent to kill themselves, but that means 31 percent did not.[35] The church cannot be responsible for suicidal thinking they were not aware of.

Also, the church is not responsible for knowing how to help if they do not know how to help. As I say often to my clients and students, you can't know something that you don't know. Once you understand your need to know, then get that knowledge. Until then, you are not guilty of not knowing.

Sabbath-Taking

Dealing with suicide is stressful. One study of 480 caregivers found that those who worked with people with current suicidal thinking or with at least one suicide attempt in their history reported "lower general health scores than caregivers associated with patients with neither of these indices."[36] Whether you are a pastor or a congregant, helping in the context of suicide is stressful because of the high stakes of life and death. How do we deal with that stress?

Many people deal with stress with a rubber band approach: stretch, stretch, stretch until we snap. But we must do what God tells us to do: practice the Sabbath (Exod 10:8). Just as God worked and then took a Sabbath rest (Gen 2:2–3), so God commands us to practice Sabbath rest (Exod 20:8–11) and invites us to come apart from the bustle of life (Mark 6:31). We come apart to pray, as Jesus regularly did (Luke 5:16), and to care for our bodies. Paul tells us, "After all, no one ever hated their own body, but they feed and care for their body, just as Christ does the church—for we are members of his body" (Eph 5:29-30). As my colleague Dr. Dave Currie is fond of saying, no one is exempt from the fourth commandment. A regular regimen of Sabbath-taking is important to every human.

How do people take a Sabbath? Pastors have told us that early in their careers they ignored their own needs and might have felt guilty saying "no" to a need. Later in their career, they understood that there will always be a person in need, and it is important to not sacrifice yourself and your family

---

34. Robins, *Final Months.*

35. Robins, *Final Months,* 410.

36. Chessick et al., "Current Suicide Ideation," 482.

to meet every need.[37] Ray Anderson advises pastors to not let human need dictate their choices. He writes,

> Human need is an insatiable and unforgiving slave master, as many pastors have found. Those who seek help from ministers as well as from other Christians will inevitably create a burden too great for any one person to bear. The double bind in using need to define one's ministry as a servant is complicated by the concept of a "calling," or vocation. My own sense of calling to be a minister was directly linked with a pastoral role that I understood as being available and on call for any person who had expressed need for counsel, comfort, advice, or simply a listening ear.[38]

As Ray Anderson points out, a rubber band approach is untenable: stretch, stretch, stretch until we snap.

Instead, we need to infuse our lives with the rhythm of Sabbath. One way to do that is to set aside a time of Sabbath to do something relaxing. When we think of relaxation, we might think of flopping on the couch. But that doesn't heal one's body from stress. Rather, we need to activate our body's natural *relaxation response*,[39] a state of deep rest that puts the brakes on stress, slows our breathing and heart rate, lowers our blood pressure, and brings our body and mind to an unstressed state. What works for one person won't work for another, so it may take some trial and error to find what works for each person. Prayer and meditation on Scripture can elicit the relaxation response.[40] Moderate exercise can help protect against the effects of stress.[41] Part of a church's approach to preventing suicide must include regular Sabbath-keeping. Allowing volunteers to take a break from their ministry is part of Sabbath-taking. Not doing so is to put Christians at risk of becoming depressed themselves,[42] which is a risk factor for suicidal thinking.[43]

---

37. Mason et al., "Developmental Model."

38. Anderson, *Soul of Ministry*, 81

39. Esch et al., "Therapeutic Use of the Relaxation Response."

40. Esch et al., "Therapeutic Use of the Relaxation Response."

41. Gerber et al., "Do Exercise and Fitness Buffer against Stress?"; see also "Exercising to Relax."

42. Hammen, "Stress and Depression."

43. Franklin et al., "Risk Factors for Suicidal Thoughts."

Pastor Suicide

Pastors may have a particular responsibility to take regular Sabbaths because helping congregants (including suicidal congregants) requires Sabbath-taking. One of our pastor study participants asked, "How do you regroup . . . when you engage a lot of suffering? And particularly when you don't feel like you're making much progress against suffering?"[44]

Pastors are affected by suicide and may need to reach out for help for themselves.[45] A pastor told us that pastors need debriefing after a suicide, the same as first responders.[46] They also need to give themselves permission to be human. As one pastor told us in an interview, "The pastor is supposed to have it all together. . . . [With this expectation] we are not helping pastors be more healthy." In a recent study, we found that five out of 131 future faith leaders said they have attempted suicide.[47] These future faith leaders need to be vulnerable and reach out for help. Not doing so will not help their churches to be more vulnerable. One of our study participants said, "[If] we are not putting [pastors] in situations where they can be vulnerable, their churches won't be."[48] Another study participant recognizes that pastors need to have "permission to weave in their own personal struggles much like David did in the Psalms."[49]

But pastors also need to recognize the unique stress of being a pastor. Duke Divinity School's Clergy Health Initiative found that the rate of depression in clergy was double that of the national rate, and the rate of anxiety was even higher.[50] They found many predictors of these mental health conditions, including job stress like grief counseling, navigating competing demands of congregants, delivering a weekly sermon that opens clergy up to criticism, needing to switch roles rapidly, sense of guilt about not doing enough, and doubting one's call to ministry. A Barna study found that nearly half of US pastors struggle with depression.[51] Another study found that Protestant clergy had the highest overall

44. Mason et al., "Clergy Referral of Suicidal Individuals," 6.

45. Mason et al., "Predictors of Clergy's Ability," 38.

46. Unpublished interview from Mason et al., "How Counselors Can Help."

47. Yang et al., "Pastor Suicide."

48. Unpublished interview from Mason et al., "How Counselors Can Help."

49. Unpublished interview from Mason et al., "How Counselors Can Help."

50. Proeschold-Bell et al., "Using Effort-Reward Imbalance Theory."

51. Kinnaman and Lyons, *Good Faith*, 246–47.

work-related stress and were next to the lowest in personal resources to cope with the occupational strain.[52]

When you add the rates of depression in pastors to pastors being put on a pedestal by their congregants,[53] the effect can be lethal. When congregants (and pastors themselves!) put pastors on a pedestal, the message is that pastors are not like other people. Pastors give help but do not seek help for themselves. They have all the answers, the solutions to everyone's problems.[54] And the solution is not reaching out for help for a possible mental health condition or suicidal thinking.

In order to reduce pastor suicide, pastors must avoid over-spiritualizing their struggles[55] and vulnerably reach out for help for their mental health condition. They must refuse to get on the pedestal. My colleague, Dr. Dave Currie, likes to say, "Pastors are just like everybody else, only more so." Pastors must admit that they are human like everyone else in the congregation. Pastors must admit that, as humans, they need support as much as their congregants need support, especially for a mental health condition. Of course, the challenge is that a faith leader is both leader and part of a faith community. Mary Clark Moschella describes this challenge: "A pastor, rabbi, minister, or spiritual teacher lives in the tension between being a member of a community and one set apart from it in order to perform a leadership role."[56] The challenge of the faith leader is to be a leader *and* a human who needs support and vulnerably reaches out for help.

Seasoned pastors talk about the importance of regular meetings with an accountability group of other pastors who journey with them honestly through the challenges of ministry. It can be a challenge for pastors to be like Blind Bartimaeus (Mark 10:46–52) who refused to let pride get in the way of reaching out for help. Doing so will help address pastor suicide.

Managing copycat behavior, guilt, and taking Sabbath are key aspects to preventing further suicidal behavior. With this chapter, we have finished laying our foundation of prevention (chs. 2–4), our frame of intervention (chs. 5–6), and the installation of safety devices of postvention (chs. 7–8). In the next and final chapter, we'll see how these all fit together into a culture, not a program.

---

52. Weaver, et al., "Mental Health Issues among Clergy."

53. Zylstra, "Why Pastors Are Committing Suicide?"

54. Mason et al., "Developmental Model."

55. Mason et al., "Developmental Model."

56. Moschella, *Ethnography*, 37.

Discussion Questions

1. Have you experienced a copycat suicide attempt or death? What was your experience?

2. How does a role model's suicidal behavior influence others?

3. What is the best way for a church to monitor vulnerable people if the church has experienced a suicide?

4. Go to sprc.org/states. What is your state doing to prevent suicide? Do you have a local suicide prevention coalition in your area?

5. How does managing guilt and engaging in regular Sabbath-keeping prevent more suicides?

Taking Stock of Your Church

1. Which people in your church do you suspect are most vulnerable to copycat suicide?

2. What would a response protocol following a suicide at your church include?

3. How could your church become involved in your state's and community's suicide prevention efforts?

4. How could your church manage guilt following a suicide?

5. Does your church have enough volunteers to allow people to take a Sabbath rest from their ministry?

6. What is your own Sabbath-taking regimen? Is it adequate to manage stress?

Resources

Avis, Fe Anam. *A Second Day: A Hopeful Journey out of Suicidal Thinking*. Columbus: Magi, 2014.

Gibson, Scott, and Karen Mason. *Preaching Hope in Darkness: Help for Pastors in Addressing Suicide from the Pulpit*. Bellingham: Lexham, 2020.

Mason, Karen. *Preventing Suicide: A Handbook for Pastors, Chaplains and Pastoral Counselors*. Downers Grove: InterVarsity, 2014.

988 Suicide & Crisis Lifeline. https://988lifeline.org/

CHAPTER 9

Essential Element 8: A Culture, Not a Program

> They devoted themselves to the apostles' teaching and to fellowship, to the breaking of bread and to prayer. Everyone was filled with awe at the many wonders and signs performed by the apostles. All the believers were together and had everything in common. They sold property and possessions to give to anyone who had need. Every day they continued to meet together in the temple courts. They broke bread in their homes and ate together with glad and sincere hearts, praising God and enjoying the favor of all the people. And the Lord added to their number daily those who were being saved. (Acts 2:42–47)

Jeff Elhart has his own experience with depression. But the turning point of his life happened when his best friend, business partner, and brother, Wayne, took his life on March 27, 2015, after a brief episode of depression. Wayne was an excellent people manager because of his honesty, reliability, and fairness to employees. The turmoil of the auto industry during the Great Recession (2009–2010) triggered depression. Wayne lost weight, his positive attitude and confidence, and he isolated himself. In the midst of depression, Wayne received Jesus Christ as his Savior shortly before his death.

After Wayne's suicide death, Jeff struggled with shock, guilt, and anger. Questions nagged him, "How had I not noticed how much he was struggling?"[1] Jeff describes himself as "a fix-it guy." He doesn't like to focus on his story but on the solution. He wants to prevent suicide from happening to anyone else. He began searching for a "simple tool"[2] to equip everyday people to prevent suicide, something like "Stop, Drop, and Roll."

---

1. Buck et al., *be nice.*, 14.
2. Buck et al., *be nice.*, 17.

During this time, Wayne's wife found a note Wayne had written before he died, "I love you all. This depression has gotten the best of me. Do not blame yourself as it was me. Please use my illness to help others. God, please help me to help others."[3] Helping others became Jeff's mission and Jeff "put things in overdrive."[4] He started with his church because "the first place you go to is the church." Jeff says that his church wasn't predisposed to a culture of suicide prevention because the church is "full of people who aren't going to let anyone know what's happening in their personal life." But Jeff's pastor, Jim Liske, believed, "If anyone should be talking about [mental illness], it should be the churches" because the Bible addresses mental health struggles.

Jeff began by bringing a suicide prevention movie, *Hope Bridge*,[5] to a packed church of 1,200 people. That opened up the conversation about suicide. While planning the event, he met Christy Buck, executive director of the Mental Health Foundation of West Michigan (MHF). That's when Jeff found the tool be nice., which Christy had developed. He teamed up with MHF and threw himself into initiating the Wayne Elhart be nice. memorial fund and raising almost $2 million in four years. These funds enable the MHF to train schools, businesses, and churches in be nice. It took a few years after *Hope Bridge* to "convince" his church to consider doing a sermon series during Mental Health Awareness Month (in May), but Jeff persevered and brought be nice. to his church, Christ Memorial Church, Holland, Michigan. be nice. is now in over fifty churches and over 150 schools and is going into businesses.[6]

The early church had a culture of unity and love for each other. What is striking is that they seemed to have had a culture, not a program. How would a church today model their approach to suicide prevention on the early church's focus on culture? How would a church offer congregants a

3. Buck et al., *be nice.*, 18.

4. Buck et al., *be nice.*, 19.

5. See also www.Speak2Save.org.

6. Author interview with Jeff Elhart, March 22, 2021. Elhart is a mental health and suicide prevention advocate at the local, regional and national levels. He owns Elhart Automotive Campus in Holland, Michigan, a second-generation automobile dealership. Elhart Automotive was the first business to implement be nice. He serves on the executive committee of the National Action Alliance for Suicide Prevention and is on two task force committees: the Faith Communities Task Force and the Workplace Task Force. He has served as Chairman of the Mental Health Foundation of West Michigan board and has served in numerous church leadership positions. He is co-author with Christy Buck of *be nice.: 4 Simple Steps to Recognize Depression and Prevent Suicide*.

community characterized by the gospel? In this chapter, we'll look at what it means to have a culture of suicide prevention, not a program.

Why Is a Suicide Prevention Program a Problem?

Pastors and congregants have told us there are many obstacles to starting a suicide prevention program. One is that they don't know what to do. One study participant said, "There are people that are aware and want to do something, and their hearts are in the right place. They just don't know what to do."[7] Some wonder whose responsibility is suicide prevention; surely, it is not the church's job! A study participant said, "[Suicide prevention] is not our job."[8] A third obstacle is not knowing how suicide intervention intersects with a mental health ministry. A study participant said, "Mental illness is one of the low-hanging fruit which obviously leads you to suicide prevention," and another countered, "I think we've made a bit of a mistake to link up mental health problems and suicidality."[9] A last obstacle is not knowing how much to invest in suicide prevention given the "competing interests, competing priorities"[10] in churches. A study participant said, "There are a lot of competing things going on. . . . Until something happens, people don't see the need [for suicide prevention]."[11] Another added, "There are so many things that feel more urgent [than suicide]. Oftentimes it gets pushed to the back burner until it comes up, then you say, 'Ah, man! I wish I could have been more prepared for that!'"[12] This barrier of competing priorities leads to the barrier of finances. One study participant said, "Funding is always a problem."

How Can We Develop a Suicide Prevention Culture?

One way to address these barriers is to think about a *culture* of suicide prevention instead of a *program*. How would a church do that?

---

7. Mason et al., "How Counselors Can Help."

8. Mason et al., "How Counselors Can Help."

9. Mason et al., "How Counselors Can Help."

10. Mason et al., "How Counselors Can Help."

11. Mason et al., "How Counselors Can Help."

12. Mason et al., "How Counselors Can Help."

A starting point is that churches are involved in suicide prevention whether they think they are or not, because they organically provide a culture of connection where congregants experience a sense of belonging and mattering, hear life-affirming teaching, and experience communal worship. Because churches provide these organically, they are helping to save lives with little investment of time and resources. However, churches need to make at least some investment of time and resources to foster a stigma-free community allowing for the safe, confidential disclosure of suicidal thinking, a skilled, equipped community, equipped with a model of suicide intervention in order to increase the skill of pastors and con-gregants to help a suicidal person, a well-networked church connected to local community resources, and a church that ministers to survivors and monitors contagion. But how is investing time and resources in suicide prevention a *culture* instead of a *program*?

A culture is a way of life. It's the character of the church. It is what brings the church together and defines the church. Culture gives the church a certain identity. A church's culture is broader than its programs. As we saw in chapter 1, an example of culture is anything that a church does that promotes health and flourishing, or *shalom*.

In order to prevent suicide, a church needs a culture of listening to each other's struggles. In chapter 2, (former) Pastor Fe advised that becoming a ministering church requires that a church develop "core com-petencies" or a basic "therapeutic capacity" of being able to listen to each other. These capacities would allow conversations about stigmatized is-sues like suicide or addictions, or systemic issues like racism. He writes, "The church is ideally positioned to address [suicide]. It does not require capital expansion, new sound systems, or changes in worship format. What it requires is conversion: a basic emotional/spiritual reorientation of the community."[13] This is a culture, not a program.

Pastor Scott (see ch. 3) said that a church reaches out to others because the church "has understood hurt and pain, and they've come to terms with it as a church. They know people aren't perfect." That perspective allows an authentic transparency where congregants dealing with a whole host of stigmatized issues beyond suicide, issues like anxiety, financial difficul-ties, or parenting challenges, would feel safe to reach out for help. A "deep community"[14] is willing to be transparently authentic. A study participant

13. Avis, *Second Day*, 115.

14. Unpublished interview from Mason et al., "How Counselors Can Help."

helped me understand what Pastor Scott said. This safety comes in foster-ing "a layer of vulnerability," as another study participant said,

> [Asking for prayer] shows a layer of vulnerability, a layer of hon-esty. I think it shows that we're not hiding things from each other, like everything's perfect . . . When people ask for prayer, it is one step towards showing people that, "Hey, I'm not perfect," and we still support them and accept them.[15]

A pastor who participated in one of our studies asked,

> How do we provide opportunities for people to connect and for those relationships to deepen to where you can be transparent? You can trust this person with your story because you have known him or her long enough and you know his character. This person is trustworthy.[16]

Jeff adds,

> Building a community that cares for one another is what church is all about. So the more we can embrace one another through a small group where we get to know one another, we identify those [suicide] warning signs. . . . Small groups, regardless of what size of the church, can really continue to play a big part in of suicide prevention because if we know one another, it's a little easier to have that conversation.

This is a culture, not a program.

Pastor Talitha (from ch. 4) explains that suicide prevention is a culture, not a program, because it is woven into the fabric of the church throughout the year. She says,

> Sometimes you can set aside specific days or Sundays for suicide prevention, but I also think that the approach needs to be woven into the other fifty-one Sundays a year. The same thing is true with the mental health issues. It's not just "one and we're done once a year," but part of the fabric of the congregation's life and ministry.

Jeff emphasizes the importance of culture. He says, "be nice. is not a program. It is far from a program. I don't like using the word 'program' because it's not. It's our culture." Jeff walked me around the Elhart Auto-motive Campus in Holland, Minnesota, and everyone he asked could say

15. Mason et al., "Unique Experiences in Religious Groups."

16. Unpublished interview from Mason et al., "How Counselors Can Help."

what be nice. stands for (with be nice. signage everywhere—even a be nice. flag flown below the American flag). This common language fosters a culture of connection. Christy Buck and Jeff Elhart provide examples of this culture[17] in a testimonial for be nice:

> be nice. has had an immense positive impact on the culture and environment here. The goal is to erase the stigma of mental health so we can talk openly about any issues and have a safe and non-judgmental place to openly share and ask for help. Another byproduct of having be nice. on campus is that it brings coworkers closer together, which promotes better teamwork and a healthier place to work.[18]

Jeff explains the importance of culture: "We can all go to an eight-hour seminar, but it goes on the shelf. You have to live [be nice.]. You have to breathe it." Jeff adds, "The more and more you make be nice. present and visible within the church, the more it becomes part of the culture."

Jeff's vision is for the whole community to have "a common language and a culture of connection," not just in schools, businesses, and churches.[19] Jeff is partnering with MHF to foster an environment that normalizes noticing, inviting, challenging, and empowering.[20] Jeff adds, "Imagine that a kindergartner today who hears about be nice. will have twelve years of this culture." He adds,

> Imagine a community where a young couple sends two students to school, where they are receiving be nice. education. They both work at a business and be nice. is part of their action plan, or they live in a retirement community and they receive be nice. education. And everybody [in the community] speaks the same language. I don't think that's too much to ask because everybody knows what "Stop, Drop, and Roll" is.

A culture of suicide prevention is a culture of "meeting people where their problems are."[21] This culture not only helps prevent suicide but addresses a whole host of human problems. A stigma-free church with "therapeutic capacity" and "deep community"[22] would allow congregants to reach out

17. Buck et al., *be nice.*, 147.
18. Buck et al., *be nice.*, 187.
19. Buck et al., *be nice.*, 145.
20. Buck et al., *be nice.*, 159.
21. Unpublished interview from Mason et al., "How Counselors Can Help."
22. Unpublished interview from Mason et al., "How Counselors Can Help."

for help for issues like depression or interpersonal violence. Life-affirming teaching could help people choose life in the context of a life-threatening illness. A model of suicide intervention would equip congregants to reach out to congregants in distress in the midst of a natural disaster. Ministering to people with complicated grief could apply to helping people who are grieving many types of losses; for example, sudden infant death syndrome. Monitoring vulnerable people in the congregation could apply to any copycat behaviors like drug use, not just copycat suicide. This is a culture, not a program.

Jeff has found that be nice. applies much more broadly than just to suicide prevention because of the interrelationship between suicide and mental illness, domestic violence, sexual abuse, and substance abuse. All these human struggles are woven together because be nice. is noticing any issue. He says, "Those are the major issues in any community." Jeff adds that mental health is a community concern in many American communities. He explains,

> In Michigan, we have a CHIP [Community Health Improvement
> Plan], and every three years in each county, we are required to do
> an assessment. That information was put up on the screen [during
> the church service] and shared with the church members to say
> that the number one issue in our county was mental health.

Why should the church have a culture of "meeting people where their problems are"?[23] Why should the church focus on the entire range of human suffering? The early church met more than just spiritual needs. The apostles healed a man paralyzed from birth (Acts 3:2). They sold possessions "to give to anyone who had need" (Acts 2:45). Early church Christians stayed in the cities to care for those affected by pandemics.[24] If a church supported each other the way the early church supported each other, then the church would help people struggling with a wide range of human problems. As Dr. Bishop C. Guy Robinson said in chapter 6,

> If we don't meet this [mental health] need, this need will be met
> in other ways. If we don't create ministry that does it, and put it in
> the context of ministry, in an increasingly secular society, then we
> may raise a generation that goes to brunch, sees their therapist,
> and never comes in our sanctuaries.

23. Unpublished interview from Mason et al., "How Counselors Can Help."

24. Stark, "Epidemics, Networks, and the Rise of Christianity," 166.

Many pastors agree with Bishop Robinson. And some believe that "mental health is the mission field of this generation."[25] Jeff asks, "If we're going to walk away from that, as a kingdom of God, what are we doing? That's our job. . . . Where there's trouble, we need to run to it."

What Do We Know about Shifting Culture?

Your church is on board. You would like to implement a culture of suicide prevention, with a foundation of prevention, a frame of intervention, and safety features of postvention. How do you get started?

Focus on what the church is already organically providing: a connected community, life-affirming teaching, and communal worship. These are all elements of a church's culture.[26] As we saw in chapter 1, flourishing activities happen in churches organically and they increase psychological well-being, and decrease depression.[27] These are elements of a church culture. But a church must also challenge stigma so that suicidal congregants can reach out for help (prevention), be equipped for intervention (being ready to help a suicidal person and connect them to community resources), and postvention (being ready to minister to loss survivors and to monitor those vulnerable to copycat suicide). Instead of a program which may come and go, intentional suicide prevention activities must be woven into the fabric of the church. Otherwise, a church may resist because "We have too much on our plate already."[28]

How Do You Shape Your Church's Culture?

Culture shift is messy and non-linear. Change doesn't happen in a neat order. You will cycle through these aspects of change many times. Generally, Jeff lays out culture shift. He said,

25. Gibson and Mason, *Preaching Hope in Darkness*, 121.

26. See chs. 1–4 for more detail about churches helping congregants flourish in their lives and consult the following: Diener et al., "Subjective Well-Being"; Emmons and McCullough, "Counting Blessings versus Burdens"; Otake et al., "Happy People Become Happier through Kindness"; Ryff, "Happiness Is Everything, or Is It?"; Seligman et al., "Positive Psychology Progress"; Sheldon et al., "Personal Goals and Psychological Growth"; Sheldon and Lyubomirsky, "How to Increase and Sustain Positive Emotion"; VanderWeele, "Activities for Flourishing."

27. Bolier et al., "Positive Psychology Interventions."

28. Unpublished interview from Mason et al., "How Counselors Can Help."

Number one, we can't talk about suicide prevention without an action plan. You need something of substance that people can get behind. Number two, you've got to have leadership behind it. Three, you have to develop a core of champions within the church that embrace it.

Let's look at these pieces.

Pastors Lead through Vulnerability

Pastors lead culture shift. They shape the church's culture. Carroll writes that

> Clergy give shape to a congregation's particular way of being a congregation. . . . Through the core work of the pastoral office—preaching, leading worship, teaching, providing pastoral care, and giving leadership in congregational life—a pastor helps to "produce" or at least decisively shape a congregation's culture.[29]

Pastors also lead by example. As Bishop Robinson (ch. 6) said, the congregation learns by watching the pastor lead in "the fish bowl." One example pastors may provide is vulnerability. As another study participant said, "Whether we like it or not, the pastor is the rock star of the concert and, the more they share, the more permission is given to be honest about [suicidal thinking]."[30] Pastors shape the church's culture by reaching out for help for themselves. While challenging, reaching out may be a life-or-death decision that pastors need to make. This is one way pastors lead the way in establishing a culture of vulnerability and safety for suicidal congregants. The pastor "breaks the silence" about depression and suicidal thinking. Jeff adds that even if this happens only once a year, "people will remember it's okay [to be honest about their own issues]."

However, Dr. Everett Worthington from Virginia Commonwealth University has found that preaching one sermon produces only a small amount of culture shift. To promote lasting culture shift, add one of these approaches:[31]

---

29. Carroll, *God's Potters*, 25.

30. Mason et al., "How Counselors Can Help."

31. These ideas are based on the forgiveness work of Dr. Everett Worthington. See his website: http://www.evworthington-forgiveness.com/.

1. Preach to motivate congregants to get involved in a more time-intensive program like a four-week Sunday School series. In the first week, raise awareness of suicide stigma (ch. 2). In week two, discuss how to be a caring community where suicidal people can reach out for help (ch. 2). In weeks three and four, teach a model of intervention like LivingWorks Start[32] or safeTALK[33] or be nice.[34] and provide information on your church's "network of safety" (see chs. 5–6).

2. Preach a sermon series on suicide.[35] In the first week, preach on Elijah's desire to die (1 Kgs 19:4). It is powerful modeling if the preacher includes their own experience with suicide or has a congregant share about their experience. In the second week, preach on reasons for living. Some people in pain have not desired death: Job (Job 2:10), Joseph (Gen 39:20), and Hannah (First Samuel 1). God is a God of hope who intervenes in hopeless situations (Gen 50:20). In the third week, preach on suffering, how Christians suffer, and how others come alongside them. Christians throughout the ages have been involved in alleviating human suffering.

3. Include a Five-Second Fix[36] at every service for six months, saying, "Christians reach out for help and help each other. How can you reach out for help this week?" One of our participants said his pastor always begins the service with: "Welcome to . . . Church, where none of us is perfect and all of us are in need of grace."[37] Pastor Scott from chapter 3 recommends: "We are a people of hope." Another study participant saw a church begin a service by asking everyone who had a panic attack this past week to stand.[38] The study participant was surprised at how many people stood and was struck by the freedom given in that moment "to share anything in that church."[39]

---

32. https://www.livingworks.net/start-usa.

33. https://www.livingworks.net/safetalk.

34. https://www.benice.org/.

35. Pastor Jim preached on Psalm 6 (David), First Kings 19 (Elijah), Jeremiah 20 (Jeremiah), and Luke 10 (the Good Samaritan). For other ideas, consult Gibson and Mason, *Preaching Hope in Darkness.*

36. Everett Worthington, personal communication with author, October 12, 2020.

37. Unpublished interview from Mason et al., "How Counselors Can Help."

38. Unpublished interview from Mason et al., "How Counselors Can Help."

39. Unpublished interview from Mason et al., "How Counselors Can Help."

Congregants Are Crucial

Congregants are crucial for culture shift. Congregants need to lead the way, too. They can be the first to be vulnerable. One study participant said, "The greatest obstacle is courage to be that first person that raises their hand and says, 'I have anxiety or I have depression and I am thinking of suicide.'"[40]

CHANGE CHAMPIONS

Another crucial job of congregants in creating a culture that prevents suicide is to find champions for change, passionate people who share the vision for suicide prevention. You will need buy-in on the culture shift from a critical mass of people who are "informal networkers"[41] or "change champions" or "evangelists for the change." To select your change champions, select people who are respected in the church and who are involved in several ministries at the church, whose influence is broad. Have informal and formal discussions as a group. Discuss your vision for your church culture. Write out a vision statement. For example, "Our church is a safe place where suffering people can reach out for help with any problem." Jeff's vision was a church equipped with a common, simple language like "Stop, Drop, and Roll," so that congregants could intervene in the struggle of a suicidal person. His vision has expanded beyond the church to schools and businesses.

Discuss each chapter of this book, especially the section at the end of each chapter called "Taking Stock of Your Church." Compare your church's current practices to your vision statement. List where your church needs to change its practices in order to align with the vision. Reflect on the barriers to making this change. Then develop an action plan, which will include an intervention model (like Soul Shop in ch. 2 or LivingWorks trainings in ch. 5 or be nice. in this chapter). Changing everything all at once is impractical. According to a wise saying attributed to Desmond Tutu, "There is only one way to eat an elephant: a bite at a time." Take a few bites, but don't try to eat the whole elephant right now. Be patient with the process of change.

40. Mason et al., "How Counselors Can Help."
41. Senge, "Rethinking Leadership."

Education and Training

Simultaneously with selecting change champions, you need to get education or training on suicide prevention. Jeff says that without knowledge, people don't have the confidence to take action. Education and training are important early on in the change process. Change champions need information to share with church leadership, information such as one out of five Americans has a mental health condition.[42] Jeff suggests getting the knowledge to be able to challenge your church leadership to "think about the possibilities within the four walls of this church of what kind of impact we can have." He adds, "It starts with education; education is the basis of everything." Rev. Dr. Dennis Goff, director of ministry programs at the Lutheran Foundation in Fort Wayne, Indiana, agrees: "[Churches need to focus on] Awareness, Education, Resources and Action."[43] Consider joining a Soul Shop or Living Works or be nice. training. One place to get facts and statistics about suicide is the American Association of Suicidology's Facts and Statistics.[44] Or you can read a book on suicide prevention.[45]

Leadership and Volunteers

After getting education, it is essential that the church's leadership is on board for culture shift. Jeff started talking with his pastoral leadership team and then the full consistory (deacons and elders). This process took a few years because "People who run churches and schools are overburdened. They don't have enough time to do the work they have. Of course, churches of less than five hundred people, the pastor is the chief bottle washer."

When you talk to your leadership, talk about the urgency of creating a culture for suicide prevention (and ministering to congregants with a broad range of human struggles). Make clear to leadership why change is needed. What are the positive consequences of making the change? (Suicidal people in the congregation will be ministered to, and lives will be saved.) What are the negative consequences of not making the change? (Suicidal congregants may feel that church is irrelevant to them, and lives may be lost.)

---

42. US Department of Health and Human Services, *Mental Health.*

43. Unpublished interview from Mason et al., "How Counselors Can Help."

44. https://suicidology.org/facts-and-statistics/.

45. E.g., Mason, *Preventing Suicide.*

What did Jeff say to the consistory? He educated them on mental health and suicide. He expected that about 20 percent of the leadership will have experienced depression, but did not expect everyone on the leadership to understand the need for change. He then provided an action plan. He said, "be nice. is just as memorable as 'Stop, Drop, and Roll.'" He found that

> [The leadership] got the message that it is very simple and could be [implemented] from the youth to the seniors in the church. The biggest asset is one common language, and it's simple. We make mental illness and suicide far more complicated than it needs to be.

As you persevere in sharing information with your leadership, look for the tipping point:[46] the point where a suicide prevention culture starts to catch on. Jeff's senior pastor, Pastor Jim Liske, had suffered with depression for a period of time in his life. Jeff says, "The challenge is if people have never felt what depression feels like, they really don't get it." Pastor Jim planned a sermon series for Mental Health Awareness Month (May). He began the series with an interview with Jeff (and interviews with others throughout the series). Each Sunday covered one of the be nice. actions: notice, invite, challenge, and empower, using Scripture like 1 Kings 19:4 (Elijah says to God, "I have had enough, LORD. Take my life").[47]

Jeff adds, "But here's the secret [to implementation]. You can't put the onus on the senior pastor or the associate pastor. It has to be volunteer led." Along with getting your leadership on board, raise up a cadre of volunteers who can do the actual implementation work.

ENLIST VOLUNTEERS

As Rev. Dr. Dennis Goff of the Lutheran Foundation, Fort Wayne, Indiana has said, "Nothing happens in a church without a pastor's support, but nothing happens in the church if the pastor is responsible [because the pastor has so many responsibilities]."[48] Jeff emphasizes that leadership is more likely to embrace change if you can show that volunteers are ready to take on needed

46. Gladwell, *Tipping Point.*

47. If you attend a be nice. training, you will be given launch materials, including sermons. Jeff and Pastor Jim wrote the curriculum for bringing be nice. into faith communities.

48. Unpublished interview from Mason et al., "How Counselors Can Help."

responsibilities. Leadership can make sure that what happens in church happens consistently across the board, but volunteers are needed to do the work.

Jeff says that the implementation of be nice. is successful in schools where the students provide the volunteer leadership through a be nice. champion team. They organize assemblies and activities at football games and signage in hallways. "They are the driving force." In the church, you have to have buy-in from the church leadership, but they have to "let go" and allow the volunteers in the church, the congregants that are passionate about this topic, to come in and take over most of the leadership. Jeff advises these passionate congregants to be persevering and organized, as they get buy-in from the top.

As we saw in chapter 4, Pastor Amy suggests pooling your church's resources with other churches in the area. She said,

> Pastors and staff are usually stretched pretty thin. . . . Time unfortunately, and sometimes money, can be a barrier. But that's where churches can pool together. There are finances out there. It's helping people creatively think through that. Every church and every community has people who have big hearts for the community and finding those resources in a community to come together to help with the funding and help with getting the word out.

Launch the Change

What Is be nice.?

We will use be nice. to illustrate launching change. But first we need to know what be nice. is. Christy Buck, LBSW, is the passionate leader of the Mental Health Foundation of West Michigan (MHF). She developed be nice. after the suicide death of Tyler Clementi following cyberbullying.[49] be nice. has been implemented in schools, businesses, and churches. Researchers at Grand Valley State University have found be nice. to be effective in increasing mental health awareness, decreasing the number of school behavioral referrals throughout the year and reducing school-wide negative behaviors.[50]

The be nice. action plan stands for:[51]

49. Buck et al., *be nice.*, 68.
50. Buck et al., *be nice.*, 67. See also Cleveland and Higbea, "be nice."
51. Buck et al., *be nice.*, 66.

- *BE* aware.

- Notice what is good and what is right about the person so that you can notice what is different. Be a detective about possible mental health issues.

- *Invite* yourself to reach out, to start a caring conversation, to listen. You can start by saying, "I've noticed that . . ."

- Challenge the stigma. Challenge the individual to seek help. Challenge yourself to ask about suicidal thinking, "Are you thinking of killing yourself?"

- *Empower* others with knowledge and resources to get help.

- *PERIOD.* It's that simple.

be nice.Faith

be nice. has been customized for churches in be nice.Faith. If your church would like to learn how to develop a culture of suicide prevention, the first step is to contact MHF[52] to attend a "What is be nice. training." Second, a be nice. liaison attends a virtual training, with up to a half a dozen people from the church. At this training, they are given all the materials the liaison will need to train their congregation, including a Faith Launch Kit (which includes a sermon series). At the training, the liaison will learn the be nice. action plan. The liaison will also learn how to build a team of five to ten members who will help plan the launch day of be nice.Faith at the church. MHF will help the liaison conceptualize the division of tasks among the launch day team members.[53] The liaison will gain access to a database of materials to sustain the culture of suicide prevention throughout the year. Jeff adds, "This database [of materials] continues to grow. [A church might say,] 'We want to do something a little different. Let's go to be nice.Faith community portal, and see what other churches have done.'"

---

52. https://www.benice.org/; https://www.benice.org/our-programs/faith.

53. Some of the team will ask local mental health practitioners to provide resources like brochures on launch day. Some of the team will make sure that information about launch day is in the church bulletin. And some will set up tables for the brochures and greet people. Some will ask mental health professionals to be there for safe pods, areas where congregants can meet with a mental health clinician following the service where *be nice.Faith* is presented.

be nice. Launch

Jeff tells the story of how his church launched be nice.:

> During that first year [on launch day], we had about eighty mem-
> bers of the church all wearing be nice. T-shirts. The full consistory
> is about sixty-five people. We asked all the consistory to be in-
> volved. The rest were volunteers. The purpose was to provide pres-
> ence and the show, if you will. This is not a fun topic to talk about.
> We made entering the church carnival-like. We had balloons
> outside. People were outside greeting with their T-shirts. It really
> presented itself as "This is a safe place. We're going to talk about
> something difficult but it's a safe place and it's a positive message."
> For four weeks, we had eighty volunteers who would greet people
> and at the end of each sermon, we had "safe pods." Throughout
> the church, we had private classrooms and we had four to eight
> counselors in those rooms and the pastor would say at the end of
> each sermon, "You may have heard something here that may have
> triggered something for you. Maybe for yourself. Maybe for your
> loved one. Maybe for your co-worker. We don't want you to leave
> here with any questions unanswered. We have these rooms, A–F.
> We encourage you to go speak with someone privately."[54]

Jeff advises not to forget young people. He shares that 50 percent of mental
illnesses exhibit by the age of 14 and 75 percent by age twenty-four. He says,
"Our church really could do a better job of engaging the youth."

Maintaining the Culture Shift

Jeff estimates that it takes three years to shape a culture, if the leadership
supports the shift. He says it's easier to maintain the shift in a business
community because churches experience changes in leadership. A new
pastor may have a different vision for the church. Jeff shares that at his
church, in the first year, congregants found be nice. interesting, but were
cautious observers: "We'll see what happens." In the second year, the congregation understood that the church is "kind of serious about this," and
in the third year, when be nice. came back, they realized, "This is part of

---

54. Pastor Jim Liske adds, "Fifty percent of those individuals who went and sat down
entered into longer term counseling situations and then there were about 15 percent who
were going on behalf of family members and they were able to get their family members
into counseling and so that safe pod idea was just a home run" (unpublished interview
from Mason et al., "How Counselors Can Help").

our culture." Jeff credits Pastor Jim Liske with keeping the focus on suicide prevention over the next three years that he was at the church. New leadership has continued to weave be nice. into the fabric of the church through the month of May each year. The church also has a permanent, staffed be nice. kiosk in the lobby and a mental health support group (called Gifts of Hope) that meets every other week.

The church's "informal networkers"[55] or "change champions" or "evangelists for the change" will help maintain the focus on the culture shift in their circles of influence. The important piece is to find ways of intentionally weaving a suicide prevention culture into the fabric of the church. A study participant said,

> It is not like, we have checked the box for suicide prevention and now we are onto the next thing. But, how we are in ongoing conversations and even in the prayers of the church, how do we let people know that we are still engaged in conversation? Because, it is not like the matter is settled. What else can we do?

A final step is to monitor how the changes are going. One way to do that is through a formal evaluation. Jeff shares that at his church, they surveyed the congregation before the sermon series and two weeks after the last sermon on be nice. He says, "What we're most proud of, two weeks after the last sermon, six weeks after the first one, 63 percent of the people could remember what NICE stood for. Two-thirds had retention of that." Monitoring change can also be informal. Talk to your change champions about what is working and what is not. Be ready to change your plan as you get more information about what works and what doesn't work at your church.

Conclusion

This book has laid out a plan for how a church can help prevent suicide. The church is crucial to suicide prevention. It provides protective elements that no one else provides, like moral reasons to stay alive and a "deep community"[56] that cares for people through prevention, intervention, and postvention. Suicide prevention is doable at your church. This is not the province of experts. This is the province of everyone in the church. Everyone has a role to play.

55. Senge, "Rethinking Leadership."

56. Unpublished interview from Mason et al., "How Counselors Can Help."

You can implement any of these suggestions in the book by themselves or all the suggestions as a whole. But you don't have to implement every suggestion. The important thing is to get started. Changing everything all at once is impractical. Start somewhere. I wish you well on your journey to preventing suicide in your church.

Discussion Questions

1. Why would fostering a suicide prevention *culture* be more successful at your church than building a suicide prevention *program*?

2. Why is one sermon per year ineffective in fostering change?

Take Stock of Your Church

1. Which of these obstacles exist in your church and how would you address them? (a) Not knowing how to do suicide prevention; (b) not knowing whose responsibility is suicide prevention; (c) not knowing how suicide intervention intersects with a mental health ministry; and (d) not knowing how much to invest in suicide prevention given the "competing interests, competing priorities"[57] in churches.

2. What is your vision statement for your church?

3. Who are potential change champions at your church?

4. In looking at the Soul Shop, LivingWorks, and be nice. trainings, which educational model resonates with you and would resonate with your church? Why?

5. What would your church leadership need to hear in order to get on board with a suicide prevention culture?

6. When would be a good launch day for your church? World Suicide Prevention Day? The National Action Alliance Faith.Hope.Life Day of Prayer? Mental Health Awareness Month?

7. Pick three of the suggestions in this chapter for implementing a suicide prevention culture and discuss: (1) why these elements are important, (2) how they are doable in your church, and (3) how you would implement them.

57. Mason et al., "How Counselors Can Help."

8. Review your answers for the "Take Stock of Your Church" sections at the end of each chapter in this book. Summarize your answers. What are the key themes? From the key themes, pick five goals for your church and develop a plan for how to implement the five goals over the next year.

9. How would you weave a suicide prevention culture into the life of your church?

Resources

Buck, Christy, and Jeff Elhart. *be nice.: 4 Simple Steps to Recognize Depression and Prevent Suicide.* Grand Rapids: Mental Health Foundation of West Michigan, 2021.

Gibson, Scott, and Karen Mason. *Preaching Hope in Darkness: Help for Pastors in Addressing Suicide from the Pulpit.* Bellingham: Lexham, 2020.

Mason, Karen. *Preventing Suicide: A Handbook for Pastors, Chaplains and Pastoral Counselors.* Downers Grove: InterVarsity, 2014.

988 Suicide & Crisis Lifeline. https://988lifeline.org/

If your church's discussion group needs consultation, contact someone from the following list:

Glen Bloomstrom, glen.bloomstrom@livingworks.net

Jeff Elhart, jeff@elhart.com

Karen Mason, karen@mason.ch

Melinda Moore, Melinda.Moore@eku.edu

Michelle Snyder, michelle@soulshopmovement.org

Leading a Civil Conversation about Suicide

Leading a civil conversation about suicide involves several steps.

Six Steps

1. *Establish ground rules*

   Ask the participants to establish their ground rules for how to have a civil conversation, such as respectful listening and speaking, no sermons, no interrupting, no side conversations, and finding common ground.

2. *Practice staying calm*

   Lead the participants in navigating emotions in a fueled conversation. Ask them to think about a recent conflict. Once they have the conflict in mind, practice:

   - Noticing the participants' reactions

   - Taking a deep breath

   - Taking the time to decide how to respond

3. *Love and courage*

   Civil conversations require both love and courage. Ask the participants to review the verses about love and courage and reflect on how these virtues inform participants about how to have the difficult conversation about suicide.

Love

- Proverbs 10:12, "Hatred stirs up strife, but love covers all offenses."

- Proverbs 17:17, "A friend loves at all times, and a brother is born for adversity."

- Luke 6:31, "And as you wish that others would do to you, do so to them."

- John 13:35, "By this all people will know that you are my disciples, if you have love for one another."

- Romans 12:16, "Live in harmony with one another. Do not be haughty, but associate with the lowly. Never be wise in your own sight."

- 1 Corinthians 12:25, "That there may be no division in the body, but that the members may have the same care for one another."

- 1 Corinthians 16:14, "Let all that you do be done in love."

- Galatians 6:2, "Bear one another's burdens, and so fulfill the law of Christ."

- Ephesians 4:1–32, "[T]herefore, a prisoner for the Lord, urge you to walk in a manner worthy of the calling to which you have been called, with all humility and gentleness, with patience, bearing with one another in love, eager to maintain the unity of the Spirit in the bond of peace. There is one body and one Spirit—just as you were called to the one hope that belongs to your call—one Lord, one faith, one baptism, . . . Be kind to one another, tenderhearted, forgiving one another, as God in Christ forgave you."

- Ephesians 4:2, "With all humility and gentleness, with patience, bearing with one another in love."

- 1 Thessalonians 3:12, "And may the Lord make you increase and abound in love for one another and for all, as we do for you."

- 1 Thessalonians 5:15, "See that no one repays anyone evil for evil, but always seek to do good to one another and to everyone."

- 1 Timothy 1:5, "The aim of our charge is love that issues from a pure heart and a good conscience and a sincere faith."

- Hebrews 10:24, "And let us consider how to stir up one another to love and good works."

- 1 Peter 1:22, "Having purified your souls by your obedience to the truth for a sincere brotherly love, love one another earnestly from a pure heart."

- 1 Peter 3:8, "Finally, all of you, have unity of mind, sympathy, brotherly love, a tender heart, and a humble mind."

- 1 John 4:20, "If anyone says, 'I love God,' and hates his brother, he is a liar; for he who does not love his brother whom he has seen cannot love God whom he has not seen."

- Hebrews 13:1, "Let brotherly love continue."

- James 4:11, "Do not speak evil against one another, brothers. The one who speaks against a brother or judges his brother, speaks evil against the law and judges the law. But if you judge the law, you are not a doer of the law but a judge."

Courage

- Joshua 1:9, "Have I not commanded you? Be strong and courageous. Do not be frightened, and do not be dismayed, for the LORD your God is with you wherever you go."

- Psalm 31:24, "Be strong, and let your heart take courage, all you who wait for the LORD!"

- Psalm 56:3–4, "When I am afraid, I put my trust in you. In God, whose word I praise, in God I trust; I shall not be afraid. What can flesh do to me?"

- Proverbs 28:1, "The wicked flee when no one pursues, but the righteous are bold as a lion."

- 1 Chronicles 16:11, "Seek the LORD and his strength; seek his presence continually!"

- Ezra 10:4, "Arise, for it is your task, and we are with you; be strong and do it."

- Isaiah 41:6, "Everyone helps his neighbor and says to his brother, 'Be strong!'"

- Isaiah 41:10, "Fear not, for I am with you; be not dismayed, for I am your God; I will strengthen you, I will help you, I will uphold you with my righteous right hand."

- John 16:33, "I have said these things to you, that in me you may have peace. In the world you will have tribulation. But take heart; I have overcome the world."

- Galatians 6:9, "And let us not grow weary of doing good, for in due season we will reap, if we do not give up."

- Ephesians 6:10, "Finally, be strong in the Lord and in the strength of his might."

- 2 Timothy 1:7, "For God gave us a spirit not of fear but of power and love and self-control."

- 1 John 4:18, "There is no fear in love, but perfect love casts out fear. For fear has to do with punishment, and whoever fears has not been perfected in love."

4. *Discuss six questions about suicide*

   Ask the following questions for discussion:

   - The hard part of talking about suicide is _______.

   - The beneficial part of talking about suicide is _______.

   - What are the stories you/we tell yourself/ourselves about suicide?

   - What are your/our implicit biases, values, and beliefs about suicide?

   - What is your experience with suicide?

   - What stigmas about suicide would keep a suicidal person in our church from reaching out for help?

5. *Discuss two viewpoints*

   Divide participants into small groups. Ask each member of each small group to represent one of two viewpoints: (1) suicide is a sin and (2) suicide is a response to psychological pain and suffering. Have each small group use this template for discussing these two viewpoints:

- What is your perspective on suicide and sin?

- What are the main points of each viewpoint? What did you agree with? What did you disagree with?

- What is the common ground between the viewpoints?

- Describe your own fears about people who hold a viewpoint you *disagree* with. How do you shame or judge them or are condescending to them?

- Listen to understand. Pick a viewpoint with which you *disagree* and state it clearly and respectfully.

- Listen with empathy. Pick a viewpoint with which you *disagree* and describe how a suicidal person might be helped by it. Pick a viewpoint with which you *agree* and describe how it could cause a suicidal person pain.

6. *Debrief*

   Ask the participants how they felt the civil conversation went. Ask participants to mention one thing they will remember from the conversation.

How to Share Your Story of Suicide

Consider these five steps in preparing to share your story of suicide.

Five Steps

1. Read Fe Anam Avis's book. Make notes about what makes his story hopeful.

   Avis, Fe Anam. *A Second Day: A Hopeful Journey out of Suicidal Thinking*. Columbus: Magi, 2014.

   Make a list about what makes your story hopeful.

2. Suicide prevention consultant Fe Anam Avis advises these nest steps:[1]

   - Reflect on your story.

   - Reflect on the lessons you have learned from your experience.

   - Get clear on how you are going to help, protect, and share your Second Day. (Your Second Day is your life following suicidal despair.)

3. As you reflect on your story, check it for the following elements. Does it

   - Include hope, healing, and recovery?

   - Include resources like the 988 Suicide & Crisis Lifeline?

   - Emphasize help-seeking?

1. Avis, *Second Day*, 125.

If your story is missing one of these elements, add it.

4. Review the "Recommendations for Reporting on Suicide" at http://reportingonsuicide.org.

   As you get ready to share your story, review the recommendations for how to talk about suicide. It's important to follow these recommendations because not following them can increase the possibility of copycat suicide.

   In Vienna, Austria, nine suicides occurred from 1980 to 1984. After the press dramatically reported on a suicide in 1986, thirteen suicides occurred that year and nine others occurred in the first few months of 1987. After this epidemic of suicides, members of the media consulted with suicide experts and stopped sensationalizing suicide. Suicides in the underground decreased to three in 1989 and four in 1990.[2]

   Since then, several agencies have worked together to develop guidelines for how media should report on suicide.[3] While you are not a reporter, incorporate these recommendations in your story.

5. Tell your story. Preparing to share your story takes time. But Fe makes the point that there is great reward in the telling of your story: "Second Day persons have an opportunity to engage in one of life's most rewarding endeavors—helping people discover a life truly worth living."[4] Sharing your story will help reduce stigma about suicide and encourage suicidal congregants to reach out for help.

2. Jamison, *Night Falls Fast*, 279–80.

3. American Foundation for Suicide Prevention, Annenberg Public Policy Center, Columbia University Department of Psychiatry, National Alliance on Mental Illness (NAMI), NAMI New Hampshire, and Substance Abuse and Mental Health Services Administration all contributed to "Recommendations for Reporting on Suicide," http://reportingonsuicide.org.

4. Avis, *Second Day*, 128.

Bibliography

Abrutyn, Seth, and Anna S. Mueller. "Are Suicidal Behaviors Contagious in Adolescence?: Using Longitudinal Data to Examine Suicide Suggestion." *American Sociological Review* 79, no. 2 (2014) 211–27.

Adcock, Elver F. *Charles H. Spurgeon, Prince of Preachers.* Anderson: Gospel Trumpet, 1925.

Anderson, Ray. *The Soul of Ministry: Forming Leaders for God's People.* Louisville: Westminster John Knox, 1997.

Andriessen, Karl, et al. "Effectiveness of Interventions for People Bereaved through Suicide: A Systematic Review of Controlled Studies of Grief, Psychosocial and Suicide-related Outcomes." *BMC Psychiatry* 19, no. 49 (2019) 1–15.

———, et al. "Prevalence of Exposure to Suicide: A Meta-Analysis of Population-based Studies." *Journal of Psychiatric Research* 88 (2017) 113–20.

Appleby, Lois, et al. "Suicide within 12 Months of Contact with Mental Health Services: National Clinical Survey." *British Medical Journal Clinical Research Edition* 318, no. 7193 (1999) 1235–39.

Atran, Scott, and Joseph Henrich. "The Evolution of Religion: How Cognitive By-products, Adaptive Learning Heuristics, Ritual Displays, and Group Competition generate Deep Commitments to Prosocial Religions." *Biological Theory* 5, no. 1 (2010) 18–30.

Augustine of Hippo. *City of God.* Edited by Philip Schaff. Translated by Marcus Dods. Nicene and Post-Nicene Fathers 2. Buffalo: Christian Literature Publishing Co., 1887.

Avis, Fe Anam. *A Second Day: A Hopeful Journey out of Suicidal Thinking.* Columbus: Magi, 2014.

Baker, Jospeh O. "Social Sources of the Spirit: Connecting Rational Choice and Interactive Ritual Theories in the Study of Religion." *Sociology of Religion* 71 (2010) 432–56.

Barranco, Raymond E. "Suicide, Religion, and Latinos: A Macrolevel Study of US Latino Suicide Rates." *Sociological Quarterly* 57, no. 2 (2016) 256–81.

Bearman, Peter S., and James Moody. "Suicide and Friendships among American Adolescents." *American Journal of Public Health* 94, no. 1 (2004) 89–95.

Biebel, David B., and Suzanne L. Foster. *Finding Your Way after the Suicide of Someone You Love.* Grand Rapids: Zondervan, 2005.

Blackmore, Emma Robertson, et al. "Psychosocial and Clinical Correlates of Suicidal Acts: Results From a National Population Survey." *British Journal of Psychiatry* 192, no. 4 (2008) 279–84.

Bolier, Linda, et al. "Positive Psychology Interventions: A Meta-Analysis of Randomized Controlled Studies." *BMC Public Health* 13, no. 1 (2013) 119.

Brenner, Lisa A., et al. "Suicidality and Veterans with a History of Traumatic Brain Injury: Precipitating Events, Protective Factors, and Prevention Strategies." *Rehabilitation Psychology* 54, no. 4 (2009) 390–97.

Bridge, Jeffrey A., et al. "Association between the Release of Netflix's *13 Reasons Why* and Suicide Rates in the United States: An Interrupted Times Series Analysis." *Journal of the American Academy of Child and Adolescent Psychiatry* 59, no. 2 (2020) 236–43.

Bruffaerts, Ronny, et al. "Treatment of Suicidal People around the World." *British Journal of Psychiatry* 199, no. 1 (2011) 64–70.

Buck, Christy, and Jeff Elhart. *be nice.: 4 Simple Steps to Recognize Depression and Prevent Suicide.* Grand Rapids: Mental Health Foundation of West Michigan, 2021.

Bullock, C. Hassell. *Psalms.* Vol. 1, *Psalms 1–72.* Grand Rapids: Baker, 2015.

Burshtein, Shimon, et al. "Religiosity as a Protective Factor against Suicidal Behavior." *Acta Psychiatrica Scandinavica* 133, no. 6 (2016) 481–88.

Carnell, Edward J. *Christian Commitment: An Apologetic.* New York: MacMillan, 1957.

Carroll, Jackson W. *God's Potters: Pastoral Leadership and the Shaping of Congregations.* Grand Rapids: Eerdmans, 2006.

Catechism of the Catholic Church. 2nd ed. New York: Doubleday, 1995.

Causton, Mary, I.M. *For the Healing of the Nations: The Story of British Baptist Medical Missions, 1792–1951.* London: Kingsgate, 1951.

Centers for Disease Control and Prevention. "CDC Recommendations for a Community Plan for the Prevention and Containment of Suicide Clusters." *MMWR* 37, no. S-6 (1998) 1–12.

———. *Vitalsigns.* (2018). https://www.cdc.gov/vitalsigns/pdf/vs-0618-suicide-H.pdf.

———. "Web-Based Injury Statistics Query and Reporting System (WISQARS)." *CDC,* 2020. http://www.cdc.gov/injury/wisqars.

Cerel, Julie, et al. "How Many People Are Exposed to Suicide? Not Six." *Suicide and Life-Threatening Behavior* 49, no. 2 (2019) 529–34.

Chen, Ying, and Tyler J. VanderWeele. "Associations of Religious Upbringing with Subsequent Health and Well-Being from Adolescence to Young Adulthood: An Outcome-Wide Analysis." *American Journal of Epidemiology* 187, no. 11 (2018) 2355–64.

Chessick, Cheryl A., et al. "Current Suicide Ideation and Prior Suicide Attempts of Bipolar Patients as Influences on Caregiver Burden." *Suicide and Life-Threatening Behavior* 37, no. 4 (2007) 482–91.

Chida, Yoichi, et al. "Religiosity/Spirituality and Mortality." *Psychotherapy and Psychosomatics* 78, no. 2 (2009) 81–90.

Clemons, James T., ed. *Sermons on Suicide.* Louisville: Westminster John Knox, 1989.

Cleveland, Rosemary, and Raymond J. Higbea. "be nice.: Phase Three Executive Summary with Data Tables." *be nice.,* October 28, 2019. https://www.benice.org/uploads/images/pdfs/be-nice.-phase-three-executive-report.pdf.

Coffill, Michelle. "Fund Honors Son's Memory: Benefits Mental Health Program." *Grand Valley Magazine,* May 25, 2017. https://www.gvsu.edu/gvmagazinearchive/fund-honors-sons-memory-470.htm.

Cohen, Carl I., et al. "Racial Differences in Suicidality in an Older Urban Population." *Gerontologist* 48, no. 1 (2008) 71–78.

Cohen, Randy, et al. "Purpose in Life and Its Relationship to All-Cause Mortality and Cardiovascular Events." *Psychosomatic Medicine* 78, no. 2 (2016) 122–33. https://doi.org/10.1097/psy.0000000000000274.

Coleman, Bonnie Watson, et al. *Ring the Alarm: The Crisis of Black Youth Suicide in America*. Washington, DC: Congressional Black Caucus, 2020.

Comtois, Katherine A., et al. "Effect of Augmenting Standard Care for Military Personnel with Brief Caring Text Messages for Suicide Prevention: A Randomized Clinical Trial." *JAMA Psychiatry* 76, no. 5 (2019) 474–83.

Cook, Joan M., et al. "Suicidality in Older African Americans: Findings from the EPOCH Study." *American Journal of Geriatric Psychiatry* 10, no. 4 (2002) 437–46.

Corrigan, Patrick W. "Mental Health Stigma as Social Attribution: Implications for Research Methods and Attitude Change." *Clinical Psychology Science and Practice* 7 (2000) 48–67.

———, et al. "Familiarity with and Social Distance from People who have Serious Mental Illness." *Psychiatric Services* 52, no. 7 (2001) 953–58.

———, et al. "Prejudice, Social Distance, and Familiarity with Mental Illness." *Schizophrenia Bulletin* 27, no. 2 (2001) 219–25.

"COVID-19 Information for Specific Groups of People." *Center for Disease Control and Prevention*, March 25, 2022. https://www.cdc.gov/coronavirus/2019-ncov/need-extra-precautions/index.html.

Currie, David A. *The Big Idea of Biblical Worship: The Development and Leadership of Expository Services*. Peabody: Hendrickson, 2017. Kindle.

Diener, Ed, et al. "Subjective Well-Being: Three Decades of Progress." *Psychological Bulletin* 125, no. 2 (1999) 276–302. https://doi.org/10.1037//0033-2909.125.2.276.

Draper, John. *National Best Practices in Suicide Prevention: Lessons Learned from Crisis Hotlines*. Paper presented at the 124th American Psychological Association Annual Convention, Denver, CO, August 2016.

Durkheim, Émile. *Suicide: A Study in Sociology*. Translated by John A. Spaulding and George Simpson. New York: Free Press, 1951.

Duschek, Stefan, et al. "Dispositional Empathy Is Associated with Experimental Pain Reduction During Provision of Social Support by Romantic Partners." *Scandinavian Journal of Pain* 20, no. 1 (2019) 205–09.

Eclov, Lee. *Pastoral Graces: Reflections on the Care of Souls*. Chicago: Moody, 2012.

Edlund, Mark J., et al. "Religiosity and Decreased Risk of Substance Use Disorders: Is the Effect Mediated by Social Support or Mental Health Status?" *Social Psychiatry and Psychiatric Epidemiology* 45, no. 8 (2009) 827–36.

Ellison, Christopher G., et al. "The Clergy as a Source of Mental Health Assistance: What Americans Believe." *Review of Religious Research* 48, no. 2 (2006) 190–211.

Emmons, Robert A., and Michael E. McCullough. "Counting Blessings versus Burdens: An Experimental Investigation of Gratitude and Subjective Well-Being in Daily Life." *Journal of Personality and Social Psychology* 84, no. 2 (2003) 377–89. https://doi.org/10.1037//0022-3514.84.2.377.

Esch, Tobias, et al. "The Therapeutic Use of the Relaxation Response in Stress-Related Diseases." *Medical Science Monitor* 9, no. 2 (2003) RA23–34.

Eva, Amy L., and Natalie M. Thayer. "The Mindful Teacher: Translating Research into Daily Well-being." *Clearing House: A Journal of Educational Strategies, Issues and Ideas* 90, no. 1 (2017) 18–25.

"Exercising to Relax." *Harvard Health Publications*, July 7, 2020. http://www.health. harvard.edu/newsletters/Harvard_Mens_Health_Watch/2011/February/exercising-to-relax.

Eynan, Rahel, et al. "The Effects of Suicide Ideation Assessments on Urges to Self-harm and Suicide." *Crisis: The Journal of Crisis Intervention and Suicide Prevention* 35, no. 2 (2014) 123–31.

Farrell, Jennifer L., and Deborah A. Goebert. "Collaboration between Psychiatrists and Clergy in Recognizing and Treating Serious Mental Illness." *Psychiatric Services* 59, no. 4 (2008) 437–40.

Fedden, Henry R. *Suicide: A Social and Historical Study.* London: Peter Davies Limited, 1938.

Fink, David S., et al. "Increase in Suicides the Months after the Death of Robin Williams in the US." *Plos One* 13, no. 2 (2018) e0191405.

Finstuen, Andrew S. *Original Sin and Everyday Protestants: The Theology of Reinhold Niebuhr, Billy Graham, and Paul Tillich in an Age of Anxiety.* Chapel Hill: University of North Carolina Press, 2009.

Fischer, Ronald, et al. "How Do Rituals Affect Cooperation?: An Experimental Field Study Comparing Nine Ritual Types." *Human Nature* 24, no. 2 (2013) 115–25.

Franklin, Joseph C., et al. "Risk Factors for Suicidal Thoughts and Behaviors: A Meta-analysis of Fifty years of Research." *Psychological Bulletin* 143, no. 2 (2017) 187–232.

Fuist, Todd Nicholas. "Talking to God among a Cloud of Witnesses: Collective Prayer as a Meaningful Performance." *Progressive Religion* 54 (2015).

Gerber, Markus, et al. "Do Exercise and Fitness Buffer against Stress among Swiss Police and Emergency Response Service Officers?" *Psychology of Sport and Exercise* 11 (2010) 286–94.

Gesundheit, Benjamin. "Suicide: A Halakhic and Moral Analysis of Masekhet Semahot, Chapter 2, Laws 1-6." *Tradition* 35, no. 3 (2001) 31–51.

Gibb, Sheree J., et al. "Mortality and Further Suicidal Behavior after an Index Suicide Attempt: a 10-year Study." *Australian and New Zealand Journal of Psychiatry* 39, no. 1–2 (2005) 95–100.

Gladwell, Malcolm. *The Tipping Point, How Little Things Can Make a Big Difference.* New York: Back Bay, 2002.

Goldstein, Pavel, et al. "Brain-to-Brain Coupling During Handholding is Associated with Pain Reduction." *Proceedings of the National Academy of Sciences* 115, no. 11 (2018) E2528–2537.

Gould, Madelyn S., et al. "Evaluating Iatrogenic Risk of Youth Suicide Screening Programs: A Randomized Controlled Trial." *JAMA* 293, no. 13 (2005) 1635–43.

———, et al. "Helping Callers to the National Suicide Lifeline who are at Imminent Risk of Suicide: Evaluation of Caller Risk Profiles and Interventions Implemented." *Suicide and Life-Threatening Behavior* 46, no. 2 (2016) 172–90.

———, et al. "National Suicide Prevention Lifeline: Enhancing Mental Health Care for Suicidal Individuals and Other People in Crisis." *Suicide and Life-Threatening Behavior* 42, no. 1 (2012) 22–35.

———, et al. "Part 2: Suicidal Crisis Callers." *Suicide and Life-Threatening Behaviors* 37, no. 3 (2007) 338–52.

Graham, Jesse, and Jonathan Haidt. "Beyond Beliefs: Religion Binds Individuals into Moral Communities." *Personality and Social Psychology* 14, no. 1 (2010) 140–50.

Gibson, Scott, and Karen Mason. *Preaching Hope in Darkness: Help for Pastors in Addressing Suicide from the Pulpit*. Bellingham: Lexham, 2020.

Global Health Metrics. "A Systematic Analysis for the Global Burden of Disease Study 2017: Global, Regional, and National Incidence, Prevalence, and Years Lived with Disability for 354 Diseases and Injuries for 195 Countries and Territories, 1990-2017." *Lancet* 392, no. 10159 (2018) 1789–1858.

Goldman, Linda. "Breaking the Silence: A Guide to Helping Children with Complicated Grief—Suicide, Homicide, AIDS, Violence and Abuse 2nd ed." New York: Taylor & Francis Group, 2001.

Goodwill, Janelle R., and Sasha Zhu. "Association between Perceived Public Stigma and Suicidal Behaviors Among College Students of Color in the US." *Journal of Affective Disorders* 1, no. 262 (2020) 1–7.

Greening, Leilani, and Laura Stoppelbein. "Religiosity, Attributional Style, and Social Support as Psychosocial Buffers for African American and White Adolescents' Perceived Risk for Suicide." *Suicide and Life-Threatening Behavior* 32, no. 4 (2002) 404–17.

Gruver, Diana. *Companions in the Darkness: Seven Saints Who Struggled with Depression and Doubt*. Downers Grove.: InterVarsity, 2020.

Haidt, Jonathan. "The Emotional Dog and Its Rational Tail: A Social Intuitionist Approach to Moral Judgment." *Psychological Review* 108 (2001) 814–34.

Haidt, Jonathan, and Craig Joseph. "Intuitive Ethics: How Innately Prepared Intuitions Generate Culturally Variable Virtues." *Daedalus* 133, no. 4 (2004) 55–66.

Hamdan, Sami, et al. "Protective Factors and Suicidality in Members of Arab Kindred." *Crisis: The Journal of Crisis Intervention and Suicide Prevention* 33, no. 2 (2012) 80–6.

Hammen, Constance. "Stress and Depression." *Annual Review of Clinical Psychology* 1 (2005) 293–319.

Harris, E. Clare, and Brian Barraclough. "Suicide as an Outcome for Mental Disorders: A Meta-Analysis." *British Journal of Psychiatry* 170 (1997) 205–28.

Harris, Keith M., and Melissa Ting-Ting Goh. "Is Suicide Assessment Harmful to Participants? Findings from a Randomized Controlled Trial." *International Journal of Mental Health Nursing* 26, no. 2 (2017) 181–90.

Hedegaard, Holly, et al. *Drug Overdose Deaths in the United States, 1999–2018: NCHS Data Brief no. 356*. Hyattsville, MD: National Center for Health Statistics, 2020.

Hilton, Sterling C., et al. "Suicide Rates and Religious Commitment in Young Adult Males in Utah." *American Journal of Epidemiology* 155, no. 5 (2002) 413–19.

Hogan, Michale F., et al. *Achieving the Promise: Transforming Mental Health Care in America: Final Report, DHHS Pub. No. SMA-03-3832*. Rockville: New Freedom Commission on Mental Health, 2003.

Hohman, Ann A., and David B. Larson. "Psychiatric Factors Predicting Use of Clergy." In *Psychology and Christianity*, Vol. 7, *Psychotherapy and Religious Values*, edited by Everett L. Worthington Jr., 71–84. Grand Rapids: Baker, 1993.

Holt-Lunstad, Julianne. "The Potential Public Health Relevance of Social Isolation and Loneliness: Prevalence, Epidemiology, and Risk Factors." *Public Policy and Aging Report* 27, no. 4 (2017) 127–30.

———, et al. "Loneliness and Social Isolation as Risk Factors for Mortality." *Perspectives on Psychological Science* 10, no. 2 (2015) 227–37.

———, et al. "Social Relationships and Mortality Risk: A Meta-analytic Review." *PLoS Med* 7, no. 7 (2010) e1000316.

Hubbard, M. Gay. *More Than an Aspirin: A Christian Perspective on Pain and Suffering.* Grand Rapids: Discovery House, 2009.

Jamison, Kay R. *Night Falls Fast: Understanding Suicide.* New York: Vintage, 1999.

Joiner, Thomas E., Jr. *Why People Die by Suicide.* Cambridge: Harvard University Press, 2005.

———, et al. *The Interpersonal Theory of Suicide: Guidance for Working with Suicidal Clients.* Washington, DC: American Psychological Association: 2009.

———, et al. "On Buckeyes, Gators, Super Bowl Sunday, and the Miracle on Ice: 'Pulling Together' Is Associated with Lower Suicide Rates." *Journal of Social and Clinical Psychology* 25, no. 2 (2006) 179–95.

Jordan, Jack, and Bob Baugher. *After Suicide Loss: Coping with Your Grief.* Newcastle, WA: Caring People, 2016.

Juth, Vanessa, et al. "Social Constraints Are Associated with Negative Psychological and Physical Adjustment in Bereavement." *Applied Psychology: Health and Well-Being* 7, no. 2 (2015) 129–48.

Kalafat, John, et al. "An Evaluation of Crisis Hotline Outcomes. Part 1: Nonsuicidal Crisis Callers." *Suicide and Life-Threatening Behaviors* 37, no. 3 (2007) 322–37.

Kaplan, Kalman J., and Matthew B. Schwartz. *A Psychology of Hope: A Biblical Response to Tragedy and Suicide.* Grand Rapids: Eerdmans, 2008.

Keefe, Rachael A. *The Lifesaving Church: Faith Communities and Suicide Prevention.* St Louis: Chalice, 2018.

Kessler, Ronald C., et al. "Trends in Suicide Ideation, Plans, Gestures, and Attempts in the United States, 1990–1992 to 2001–2003." *JAMA* 293, no. 20 (2005) 2487–95.

Kim, Eric S., and Tyler J. VanderWeele. "Mediators of the Association between Religious Service Attendance and Mortality." *American Journal of Epidemiology* 188, no. 1 (2018) 96–101.

Kinnaman, David, and Gabe Lyons. *Good Faith: Being a Christian when Society Thinks You're Irrelevant and Extreme.* Grand Rapids: Baker, 2016.

Koenig, Harold, et al. *Handbook of Religion and Health.* New York: Oxford University Press, 2012.

Kucukalic, Sabina, and Abdulah Kucukalic. "Stigma and Suicide." *Psychiatria Danubina* 29, no. 5 (2017) 895–99.

Larson, David B., and Susan S. Larson. "Spirituality's Potential Relevance to Physical and Emotional Health: A Brief Review of Quantitative Research." *Journal of Psychology and Theology* 31, no. 1 (2003) 37–51.

Law, Mary Kate, R. et al. "Does Assessing Suicidality Frequently and Repeatedly Cause Harm? A Randomized Control Study." *Psychological Assessment* 27, no. 4 (2015) 1171–81.

Lawrence, Ryan E., et al. "Religion and Suicide Risk: A Systematic Review." *Archives of Suicide Research* 20, no. 1 (2015) 1–21.

Lee, Yuri, and Kyung Ja Oh. "Validation of Reasons for Living and Their Relationship with Suicidal Ideation in Korean College Students." *Death Studies* 36, no. 8 (2012) 712–22.

Lessing, Doris. *The Golden Notebook: A Novel.* New York: Harper Perennial Modern Classics, 2008.

Li, Shanshan, et al. "Association of Religious Service Attendance with Mortality among Women." *JAMA Internal Medicine* 176, no. 6 (2016) 777–85.

———, et al. "Religious Service Attendance and Lower Depression among Women—a Prospective Cohort Study." *Annals of Behavioral Medicine* 50, no. 6 (2016) 876–84.

"Life Is for Living: A Reflection on Suicide." *Irish Catholic Bishops' Conference*, September 10, 2008. https://www.catholicbishops.ie/2008/09/10/irish-catholic-bishops-confer ence-pastoral-letter-life-living-reflection-suicide-mark-world-suicide-prevention- day/.

Linde, Katja, et al. "Grief Interventions for People Bereaved by Suicide: A Systematic Review." *PLoS One* 12, no. 6 (2017) 10.1371.

Linehan, Marsha M., et al. "Reasons for Staying Alive When You Are Thinking of Killing Yourself: The Reasons for Living Inventory." *Journal of Consulting and Clinical Psychology* 51, no. 2 (1983) 276–86.

Luther, Martin. "Table Talk: April 7, 1532." In Vol. 15, *Luther's Works*, edited and translated by Theodore G. Tappert, 29. St. Louis: Concordia, 1967.

Marshall, Doreen S. "Clergy Workgroup on Suicide Prevention and Aftercare." Newton: Educational Development Center, 2005.

Martín-María, Natalia, et al. "The Impact of Subjective Well-Being on Mortality." *Psychosomatic Medicine* 79, no. 5 (2017) 565–75.

Marty, Meghan A., et al. "Relationships among Dispositional Coping Strategies, Suicidal Ideation, and Protective Factors against Suicide in Older Adults." *Aging and Mental Health* 14, no. 8 (2010) 1015–23.

Mason, Karen. *Preventing Suicide: A Handbook for Pastors, Chaplains and Pastoral Counselors.* Downers Grove: InterVarsity, 2014.

———, et al. "Clergy as Suicide Prevention Gatekeepers." *Journal of Pastoral Care and Counseling* 75, no. 2 (2021) 84–91.

———, et al. "Clergy Referral of Suicidal Individuals: A Qualitative Study." *Journal of Pastoral Care and Counseling* 65, no. 3 (2011) 1–11.

———, et al. "Clergy Use of Suicide Prevention Competencies." *OMEGA: Journal of Death and Dying* 8, no. 3 (2020) 404–23.

———, et al. "A Developmental Model of Clergy Engagement with Suicide: A Qualitative Study." *OMEGA: Journal of Death and Dying* 79, no. 4 (2019) 347–63.

———, et al. "How Counselors Can Help Faith Communities Lower Suicide Risk: A Qualitative Study." *Counseling and Values* (forthcoming).

———, et al. "The Moral Deliberations of 15 Clergy on Suicide and Assisted Death: A Qualitative Study." *Pastoral Psychology* 66, no. 3 (2017) 335–51

———, et al. "Predictors of Clergy's Ability to Fulfill a Suicide Prevention Gatekeeper Role." *Journal of Pastoral Care and Counseling* 70, no. 1 (2016) 34–39.

———, et al. "Suicidal Ideation and Sense of Community in Faith Communities." *Religions* 9, no. 2 (2018) 40.

———. "Suicide Stigma in Christian Faith Communities, a Qualitative Study." *Religions* 12, no. 540 (2021). https://doi.org/10.3390/rel12070540.

———, et al. "Unique Experiences in Religious Groups, in the US and China: A Qualitative Study." *Mental Health, Religion and Culture* 21, no. 6 (2018) 609–24.

McCullough, Michael E., et al. "Religion, Self-Regulation, and Self-Control: Associations, Explanations, and Implications." *Psychological Bulletin* 135, no. 1 (2009) 69–93.

McMinn, Mark R., et al. "Basic and Advanced Competence in Collaborating with Clergy." *Professional Psychology: Research and Practice* 34, no. 2 (2003) 197–202, 307.

Milstein, Glen, et al. "Implementation of a Program to Improve the Continuity of Mental Health Care through Clergy Outreach and Professional Engagement (C.o.P.E.)." *Professional Psychology: Research and Practice* 39, no. 2 (2008) 218–28.

Moak, Z.B., and Arpana Agrawal. "The Association between Perceived Interpersonal Social Support and Physical and Mental Health: Results from the National Epidemiological Survey on Alcohol and Related Conditions." *Journal of Public Health* 32, no. 2 (2010) 191–201.

Morton, Kelly R., et al. "Pathways from Religion to Health: Mediation by Psychosocial and Lifestyle Mechanisms." *Psychology of Religion and Spirituality* 9, no. 1 (2017) 106–17.

Moschella, Mary Clark. *Ethnography as a Pastoral Practice: An Introduction*. Cleveland: Pilgrim, 2008.

Mościcki, Eve K. "Epidemiology of Suicide." In *The Harvard Medical School Guide to Suicide Assessment and Intervention*, edited by Douglas G. Jacobs, 40–51. San Francisco: Jossey-Bass, 1999.

Motto, Jerome A. "Suicide Prevention for High-Risk Persons Who Refuse Treatment." *Suicide: A Quarterly Journal of Life-Threatening Behavior* 6, no. 4 (1976) 223–30.

Motto, Jerome A., and Alan G. Bostrom. "A Randomized Controlled Trial of Postcrisis Suicide Prevention." *Psychiatric Services* 52, no. 6 (2001) 828–33.

Nicoletti, L.J. "Morbid Topographies: Placing Suicide in Victorian London." In *A Mighty Mass of Brick and Smoke: Victorian and Edwardian Representations of London*, edited by Lawrence A. Phillips, 7–34. London: Brill, 2007.

Niederkrotenthaler, Thomas, et al. "Exposure to Parental Mortality and Markers of Morbidity, and the Risks of Attempted and Completed Suicide in Offspring: An Analysis of Sensitive Life Periods." *Journal of Epidemiology and Community Health* 66 (2012) 232–39.

Nisbet, Paul, A., et al. "The Effect of Participation in Religious Activities on Suicide versus Natural Death in Adults 50 and Older." *Journal of Nervous and Mental Disease* 188, no. 8 (2000) 543–46.

Nonnemaker, James M., et al. "Public and Private Domains of Religiosity and Adolescent Health Risk Behaviors: Evidence from the National Longitudinal Study of Adolescent Health." *Social Science and Medicine* 57, no. 11 (2003) 2049–54.

Oquendo, Maria A., et al. "Protective Factors against Suicidal Behavior in Latinos." *Journal of Nervous and Mental Disease* 193, no. 7 (2005) 438–43.

Otake, Keiko, et al. "Happy People Become Happier through Kindness: A Counting Kindnesses Intervention." *Journal of Happiness Studies* 7, no. 3 (2006) 361–75. https://doi.org/10.1007/s10902-005-3650-z.

Ovwigho, Pamela C., et al. "Private Spiritual Practices: Bible Engagement and Moral Behavior." *Journal of Psychology and Christianity* 35, no. 3 (2016) 233–41.

Paladino, Maria-Paola, et al. "Synchronous Multisensory Stimulation Blurs Elf-Other Boundaries." *Psychological Science* 21, no. 9 (2010) 1202–07.

Pawlikowski, Jakub, et al. "Religious Service Attendance, Health Behaviors and Well-Being—an Outcome-Wide Longitudinal Analysis." *European Journal of Public Health* 29, no. 6 (2019) 1177–83.

Pennebaker, James W., et al. "Confronting a Traumatic Event: Toward an Understanding of Inhibition and Disease." *Journal of Abnormal Psychology* 95, no. 3 (1986) 274–81.

Pienaar, Jacobus, et al. "Occupational Stress, Personality Traits, Coping Strategies, and Suicide Ideation in the South African Police Service." *Criminal Justice and Behavior* 34, no. 2 (2007) 246–58.

Plantinga, Cornelius, Jr. *Not the Way It's Supposed to Be: A Breviary of Sin*. Grand Rapids: Eerdmans, 1995.

Proeschold-Bell, Rae Jean, et al. "Using Effort-Reward Imbalance Theory to Understand High Rates of Depression and Anxiety among Clergy." *Journal of Primary Prevention* 34, no. 6 (2013) 439–53.

Putnam, Robert D. *Bowling Alone: The Collapse and Revival of American Community.* New York: Simon & Schuster, 2000.

Qin, Ping. "The Relationship of Suicide Risk to Family History of Suicide and Psychiatric Disorders." *Psychiatric Times* 20, no. 13 (2003).

Ramchand, Rajeev, et al. "Characteristics and Proximal Outcomes of Calls Made to Suicide Crisis Hotlines in California: Variability across Centers." *Crisis: The Journal of Crisis Intervention and Suicide Prevention* 38, no. 1 (2017) 26–35.

Rasic, Daniel, T., et al. "Spirituality, Religion and Suicidal Behavior in a Nationally Representative Sample." *Journal of Affective Disorders* 114, nos. 1–3 (2009) 32–40.

"Release of '13 Reasons Why' Associated with Increase in Youth Suicide Rates." *National Institute of Mental Health*, April 29, 2019. https://www.nimh.nih.gov/news/science-news/2019/release-of-13-reasons-why-associated-with-increase-in-youth-suicide-rates.

Report on the National Suicide Hotline Improvement Act of 2018. Washington, DC: Federal Communications Commission, 2019.

Roberts, Daniel A. "Preparing a Eulogy or Memorial Service for One Who Died by Suicide." In *The Suicide Funeral (Or Memorial Service): Honoring Their Memory, Comforting Their Survivors*, edited by Melinda Moore and Daniel A. Robert, 12–18. Eugene, OR: Resource, 2017.

Robins, Eli. *The Final Months: A Study of the Lives of 134 Persons Who Committed Suicide.* New York: Oxford University Press, 1981.

Robinson, Haddon W. "Blending Bible Content and Life Application." In *Making a Difference in Preaching*, edited by Scott M. Gibson, 57–64. Grand Rapids: Baker, 1999.

Rostila, Mikael, et al. "Suicide Following the Death of a Sibling: a Nationwide Follow-up Study from Sweden." *BMJ Open* 3 (2013) e002618.

Rottman, Joshua, et al. "Tainting the Soul: Purity Concerns Predict Moral Judgments of Suicide." *Cognition* 130, no. 2 (2014) 217–26, 223.

Rottman, Joshua, and Liane Young. "Specks of Dirt and Tons of Pain: Dosage Distinguishes Impurity from Harm." *Psychological Science* 30, no. 8 (2019) 1151–60.

Rushing, Nicole C., et al. "The Relationship of Religious Involvement Indicators and Social Support to Current and Past Suicidality among Depressed Older Adults." *Aging and Mental Health* 17, no. 3 (2013) 366–74.

Ryff, Carol D. "Happiness Is Everything, or Is It?: Explorations on the Meaning of Psychological Well-Being." *Journal of Personality and Social Psychology* 57, no. 6 (1989) 1069–81. https://doi.org/10.1037//0022 3514.57.6.1069.

Saroglou, Vassilis. "Believing, Bonding, Behaving, and Belonging: The Big Four Religious Dimensions and Cultural Variation." *Journal of Cross-Cultural Psychology* 42, no. 8 (September 2, 2011) 1320–40.

Seligman, Martin E.P. *Flourish: A Visionary New Understanding of Happiness and Well-Being.* New York: Free Press, 2011.

———, et al. "Positive Psychology Progress: Empirical Validation of Interventions." *American Psychologist* 60, no. 5 (2005) 410–21. https://doi.org/10.1037/0003-066x .60.5.410.

Senge, Peter. "Rethinking Leadership in the Learning Organization." *Systems Thinker*, 2018. https://thesystemsthinker.com/rethinking-leadership-in-the-learning-organi zation/.

Sheldon, Kennon M., et al. "Personal Goals and Psychological Growth: Testing an Intervention to Enhance Goal Attainment and Personality Integration." *Journal of Personality* 70, no. 1 (2002) 5–31. https://doi.org/10.1111/1467-6494.00176.

Sheldon, Kennon M., and Sonja Lyubomirsky. "How to Increase and Sustain Positive Emotion: The Effects of Expressing Gratitude and Visualizing Best Possible Selves." *Journal of Positive Psychology* 1, no. 2 (2006) 73–82. https://doi.org/10. 1080/17439760500510676.

Smedes, Lewis B. "Good Question: Is Suicide Unforgiveable?" *Christianity Today*, July 10, 2000. http://www.christianitytoday.com/ct/2000/july10/30.61.html

Smietana, Bob. "1 in 3 Protestant Churchgoers Personally Affected by Suicide." *Christianity Today*, July 1, 2022. http://www.christianitytoday.com/news/channel/utilities/print. html.

Smith, Christian. "Theorizing Religious Effects among American Adolescents." *Journal for the Scientific Study of Religion* 42, no. 1 (2003) 17–30.

Spencer, Aida B., and William D. Spencer. *Joy through the Night: Biblical Resources for Suffering People*. Downers Grove: InterVarsity, 1994.

Spurgeon, C.H. "Joy and Peace in Believing no. 692." *Spurgeon Gems*, May 20, 1866. http:// www.spurgeongems.org/vols10-12/chs692.pdf.

Stack, Steven. "The Effect of the Decline in Institutionalized Religion on Suicide, 1954-1978." *Journal for the Scientific Study of Religion* 22, no. 3 (1983) 239–52.

———. "Media Coverage as a Risk Factor in Suicide." *Journal of Epidemiology and Community Health* 57 (2003) 238–40.

———. "Suicide in the Media: a Quantitative Review of Studies based on Nonfictional Stories." *Suicide and Life-Threatening Behavior* 35, no. 2 (2005) 121–33.

Stark, Rodney. "Epidemics, Networks, and the Rise of Christianity." *Semeia* 56 (1992) 159–75.

Suicide Prevention Resource Center. *After a Suicide: Recommendations for Religious Services and Other Public Memorial Observances*. Newton: Education Development Center, Inc., 2004.

Szasz, Thomas. "The Case against Suicide Prevention." *American Psychologist* 41, no. 7 (1986) 806–12.

Tajadura-Jiménez, Ana, et al. "The Other in Me: Interpersonal Multisensory Stimulation Changes the Mental Representation of the Self." *PLoS ONE* 7, no. 7 (2012). https:// doi.org/10.1371/journal.pone.0040682.

Teikmanis, Arthur L. *Preaching and Pastoral Care*. Englewood Cliffs: Prentice-Hall, 1964.

Thoits, Peggy A. "Mechanisms Linking Social Ties and Support to Physical and Mental Health." *Journal of Health and Social Behavior* 52, no. 2 (June 2011) 145–61.

Thompson, Martie P., et al. "Prospective Associations between Delinquency and Suicidal Behaviors in a Nationally Representative Sample." *Journal of Adolescent Health* 40, no. 3 (2007) 232–37.

Tybur, Joshua M., et al. "Microbes, Mating, and Morality: Individual Differences in three Functional Domains of Disgust." *Journal of Personality and Social Psychology* 97, no. 1 (2009) 103–22.

———, et al. "Disgust: Evolved Function and Structure." *Psychological Review* 120, no. 1 (2013) 65–84.

US Department of Health and Human Services. *Mental Health: A Report of the Surgeon General.* Rockville: US Department of Health and Human Services, Substance Abuse and Mental Health Services Administration, Center for Mental Health Services, National Institutes of Health, National Institute of Mental Health, 1999.

———. *2012 National Strategy for Suicide Prevention: Goals and Objectives for Action.* Washington, DC: Health and Human Services, 2012.

VanderWeele, Tyler J. "Activities for Flourishing: An Evidence-Based Guide." *Journal of Positive Psychology and Wellbeing* 4, no. 1 (2020) 79–91. https://doi.org/10.2139/ssrn.3327326.

———. "Religious Communities and Human Flourishing." *Current Directions in Psychological Science* 26, no. 5 (2017) 476–81.

———. "Religious Communities, Health, and Well-Being: Address to the US Air Force Chaplain." *Military Medicine* 183, no. 5–6 (2018) 105–09.

———, et al. "Association between Religious Service Attendance and Lower Suicide Rates among US Women." *JAMA Psychiatry* 73, no. 8 (2016) 845–51.

———, et al. "Reimagining Health—Flourishing." *JAMA* 321, no. 17 (2019) 1667.

———, et al. "Response to 'Church Attendance and Mortality.'" *American Journal of Epidemiology* 185, no. 7 (2017) 526–28.

———, et al. "Attendance at Religious Services, Prayer, Religious Coping, and Religious/Spiritual Identity as Predictors of All-Cause Mortality in the Black Women's Health Study." *American Journal of Epidemiology* 185, no. 7 (2017) 515–22.

Vandrunen, David. *Living in God's Two Kingdoms: A Biblical Vision for Christianity and Culture.* Wheaton: Crossway, 2010.

Velting, Drew M., and Madelyn S. Gould. "Suicide Contagion." In *Review of Suicidology,* Ronald W. Maris, Morton M. Silverman, and Sylvia S. Canetto, 96–137. New York: Guilford, 1997.

Vincent, Milton. *A Gospel Primer for Christians.* Bemidji: Focus, 2008.

Wang, Mei-Chuan, Y., et al. "Suicide Protective Factors in Outpatient Substance Abuse Patients: Religious Faith and Family Support." *International Journal for the Psychology of Religion* 26, no. 4 (2016) 370–81. https://doi.org/10.1080/10508619.2016.1174568.

Wang, Philip S., et al. "Patterns and Correlates of Contacting Clergy for Mental Disorders in the United States." *Health Services Research* 38, no. 2 (2003) 647–73.

Watt, Jeffrey R. *Choosing Death: Suicide and Calvinism in Early Modern Geneva.* Kirksville, MO: Truman State University, 2001.

Weaver, Andrew J., et al. "Mental Health Issues among Clergy and other Religious Professionals: A Review of Research." *Journal of Pastoral Care and Counseling* 56, no. 4 (2002) 393–403.

Willimon, William H. *Worship as Pastoral Care.* Nashville: Abingdon: 1979.

Wiltermuth, Scott S., and Chip Heath. "Synchrony and Cooperation." *Psychological Science* 20, no. 1 (2009) 1–5.

World Health Organization. *Preventing Suicide: A Global Imperative.* Geneva: World Health Organization, 2014.

Xygalatas, Dimitris, et al. "Extreme Rituals Promote Prosociality." *Psychological Science* 24, no. 8 (2013) 1602–05.

Yang, Zihan, et al. "Pastor Suicide." Forthcoming 2022.

Young, Ilanit Tal, et al. "Suicide Bereavement and Complicated Grief." *Dialogues in Clinical Neuroscience* 14, no. 2 (2012) 177–86.

Zylstra, Sarah Eekhoff. "Why Pastors Are Committing Suicide?" *Gospel Coalition*, November 23, 2016. https://www.thegospelcoalition.org/article/why-pastors-are-committing-suicide/.